Endc

"*B.A.S.I.C.* captures essential leadership principles that will help students to 'Climb On!' to their full potential as leaders. Fred's unique and inspiring perspective on leadership is refreshing, sharp, and entertaining. Students will love his stories, while educators and parents will love his practical leadership advice."

John Beede—Author, Speaker, and
World-Renowned Mountaineer

"Do you want to stand out from the pack? Then read *B.A.S.I.C.* This book is full of must-have real-world leadership training. You will learn to build your leadership confidence, competence and character."

Richard Griffin—Army Ranger

"Students today simply don't understand the importance of being under command, and instead they jockey for authority and power over their own lives. A trip to boot camp would do them good, but the next best thing is to read and listen to Army Veteran Fred Grooms. His latest book, *B.A.S.I.C.*, offers the same time-tested leadership lessons that America's bravest young leaders had to learn during their first weeks in the Army. Fred's message is a timely one that will hopefully talk some sense into a generation ready to rule the world."

Brooks Gibbs—National Social Skills Educator

"From his early days as an army officer and youth pastor, to his current training sessions and writing, Fred's focus has always been consistent…providing support and encouragement to students. That purpose comes through loud and clear in his most recent book. For any student or young adult looking for suggestions and guidance concerning the subject of leadership, my advice is simple: read *B.A.S.I.C. Student Leadership* for awareness and understanding, and apply its principles for success!"

Colonel Dave Day

"Fred is an expert communicator who offers a unique leadership perspective that students find enjoyable. *B.A.S.I.C.* is filled with practical leadership advice that every student needs to hear. This is a must-have student leadership resource."

Grant Baldwin—Motivational Speaker and Founder of The Speaker Lab

"Fred was a superior officer who served under my command, and his ability to train young soldiers was unmatched. Fred has taken his years of Army leadership experience and created a must-have hands-on leadership training manual. Every student should have the opportunity to benefit from the wisdom found within the pages of *B.A.S.I.C. Student Leadership*."

Colonel Stan Luallin

"*The Student Leadership Field Manual* should be on the required reading list for every middle school and high school that values student leadership. Fred's military officer background and his unique way of connecting with students make for a book filled with expert, no-nonsense advice and stories that will impact every reader. His B.A.S.I.C. formula is brilliant—students will undoubtedly refer to this gem for the rest of their lives!"

Ann Vertel, Ph.D.—Entrepreneur, Keynote Speaker, Executive Coach

"B.A.S.I.C. *The Student Leadership Field Manual*, is a must-read for any student who wants to learn to lead themselves and others in a positive direction. Grooms lays the foundation and describes essential characteristics that leaders must possess to succeed. His personal illustrations from his experience as an Army Veteran on the front lines demonstrate that anyone can rise and lead with the right mindset and choices. *B.A.S.I.C.* is the boot camp for aspiring young leaders."

Jeff Veley—Peace Ambassador, Golden Rule International

"Fred Grooms has gone through some of the best training in the world, and he has taken this training and applied it to student leadership. His work will help our next generation to become great leaders. I highly recommend *B.A.S.I.C.* for students and young adults who want to take their leadership skills to the next level."

Pete Vargas—CEO and Founder of Advance Your Reach

"Fred is 'right on the money' when it comes to leadership principles. I have served in both the US Marine Corps and the US Army in combat arms units, as a Drill Sergeant and trainer for soldiers from basic trainees to senior level commanders. I can attest that *B.A.S.I.C.* provides leadership training that springs from real-world experiences of influencing others. You are going to want to help your student leaders understand how the 'military way' can positively affect their leadership ability. Send your student to B.A.S.I.C. Give them a copy of the book."

SFC Sean Riley—Drill Sergeant

"Ask any US Army veteran and they will tell you that the experiences they learned from the military are invaluable. Fred successfully unpacks those lessons, especially the principles involving leadership and influence, in an easy-to-consume way. Every young person would benefit from Fred's words and thought-provoking study questions.

Erick Rheam—United States Military Academy Graduate

"Don't make the mistake of thinking this book is for people that might go into the military! Very few of the leaders we encounter today are responsible for the lives of everyone around them, have represented our entire nation abroad and are ready to sacrifice their own life for others. Any lesson that comes from that kind of leader is a lesson you better pay close attention to. Fred Grooms is that kind of leader. You need this book!"

John P. Dennis—"The Male Mentorship Guru"
and Author of *Men Raised by Women*

"Mr. Grooms has written a powerful book that I wish I had read when I was still in high school. I've found that the advice he offers in *B.A.S.I.C.* is totally true for me and my friends. The book is easy to read, and full of stories. You should really take a look at what he has to say."

Halley Barba—University Student

"In University, the faculty urges each student to take charge of their future and to lead among their classmates. However, without some sort of guidelines or reference, our generation wanders aimlessly. Mr. Grooms' book *B.A.S.I.C.* is this guideline. If only every college student were to read this, the impact it would have on them would be lifelong."

Flynn Lancaster—University Student

"*B.A.S.I.C.* is an inspirational book that every student should read. Organized in sections like a military manual, Fred's book is clear, concise, and easy to read and understand. Through the use of direct language and real-world illustrations, this manual communicates knowledge that will help students improve their leadership skills."

Kiley Haftorson—University Student

"After reading this book and having heard these words come from my father's mouth for years prior, I have come to the conclusion that *he's actually a genius.* The words and concepts of *B.A.S.I.C.* ring true in every aspect of my college life. My college leadership courses might as well be titled 'everything my dad ever taught me,' because the parallels between his teachings and those of my doctoral educators are incredible. He was preparing me for a life of leadership all those years—who knew? My dad can officially say to me 'I told you so!'"

Abby Grooms—University Student and the Author's Daughter

B.A.S.I.C.
THE STUDENT
LEADERSHIP
FIELD MANUAL

FRED GROOMS

LEADERSHIP LESSONS
FOR
EVERY STUDENT

Barnabas Consulting LLC
Blythewood, South Carolina

Fred Grooms is a popular inspirational speaker for student audiences, an educator, a two-time bestselling author, and an expert in the field of leadership. Fred has over 20 years of experience teaching students how to identify their gifts, build character, overcome any limitations, and recognize their personal and professional call to leadership.

Fred sees his success as a direct result of learning the foundational elements of leadership that are taught in the military. As a cadet in the leading Senior Military College in the nation, the University of North Georgia, he developed his personal leadership skills and strengths and learned to manage his greatest weakness—his dyslexia. Upon graduating, Fred earned a commission as an officer in the U.S. Army.

Barnabas Consulting LLC
Blythewood, South Carolina
www.fredgrooms.com

ISBN 978-0-9914628-5-8 (paperback)
ISBN 978-0-9914628-6-5 (Kindle ebook)

Printed in the United States of America

Cover design by Brian J. Halley, www.bookcreatives.com
Interior design by Jennifer Omner, www.allpublications.com

Contents

For everyone who has served or who will serve our nation.
Your service provides our freedom.

Preface

I'd like to thank you for selecting this book. It is my hope that as a student you will find the information helpful as you move forward into your future. This book is designed as a resource to assist you in understanding the foundational elements of leadership. As you progress in life, you will find yourself leading others. Leadership is inevitable. Leading others may sound exciting to you; or perhaps it sounds like a nightmare you cannot escape. Either way, you *will* be leading others, so it is imperative that you learn the basic foundational elements of leadership.

Purpose

In the pages that follow, you will find a proven approach to student leadership that will help you develop your personal leadership skills. This approach is based on the US Army's leadership philosophy, which historically has given young individuals the greatest opportunity to lead. It is a philosophy that has been battle-tested over time and has been proven to work. *The Army leadership model is a superior system that produces above average leaders from average men and women.*

With this philosophy in mind, using the official Army Leadership Field Manual, and based on my personal experience as an Army Officer and leadership trainer, I created *B.A.S.I.C. The Student Leadership Field Manual.* I have taken the Army training program on leadership and molded it in such a way that it is a student-friendly leadership formula. What the Army teaches about leadership can and should be learned by every student.

PREFACE

Often we as educators start teaching students leadership with a broad brush and with theoretical approaches. We talk about leadership styles, strategies, implementation methods, the strengths and weaknesses of leaders, and even evaluation procedures—without teaching you the very *basics* of leadership. This is a mistake; a mistake that the military philosophy does not make.

You must learn *the basic foundational elements of leadership* in order to become an outstanding leader.

It is important to note that my goal is not to recruit you to become a member of the military. The military is only right for a very few; and joining the military is a personal decision, a decision not made quickly or without the support of your family and friends.

Acknowledgments

My father, LTC. Jimmy Grooms—without his wisdom and encouragement I would not be the man I am today. He held me accountable for my behavior, attitude and choices; he set the standard for what it means to be a man of integrity. I love you Dad.

It would be impossible for me to write this book on leadership without acknowledging the military men who were my heroes and inspiration. COL. Paul Simon; LTC. Neal Lang; LTC. Seymour Levine; COL. Stan Luallin; COL. Charles Beckwith; MSG. James Williams; and MSG. Edward Jeffcoat.

This book would not have been possible without the encouragement and professional guidance I have received from Brooks Gibbs. He has guided me through the difficult process of becoming a professional speaker, and he continues to encourage me to place my faith in God above all earthly concerns.

I would also like to acknowledge John P. Dennis. His expert knowledge as an author and coach were instrumental in the development of student discussion questions.

Without the support of my wife Sarah, none of what I accomplish would be possible. She is my greatest fan. I love you Sarah.

To my daughter Abby who is my first-draft editor. It is no small task to edit my writing. Because I am dyslexic, I have to rely on someone to correct my writing errors, and my daughter takes on this difficult task willingly. I love you Abby.

To my son Eric who is willing to listen to my stories over and over. He has the difficult task of listening to every keynote speech as my test audience. You rock, son. I love you Eric.

Introduction

The Army has a long history of producing great leaders, and the Army leadership model is known to be a superior leadership training system. This system produces above-average leaders from average men and women. The military counts among its finest leaders: presidents, lawmakers, CEO's, and leaders in every civilian career. You too can be one of those leaders.

The Army philosophy of leadership is often misunderstood. When people think about Army leadership, they often envision an officer or sergeant standing before their unit shouting orders and commands to the troops, and everyone blindly following along as if they were robots. This couldn't be further from the truth.

Also, it is often thought that Army leadership is built around fear and intimidation. This is enormously inaccurate. If one were to think Army leadership is solely about *rank*, they would also be wrong. At its very core, Army leadership is about *character*, as well as motivation, quality training, shared experiences, personal skills, and accountability.

You need to understand that the Army sees an individual's *character* as well as the ability to motivate, train and maintain accountability as part of its traditional "BE, KNOW, DO" framework.

Simply put, it looks like this: a leader's character and competence is the BE; the skills of the leader are the KNOW; and the leader taking action is the DO. This framework is directly from the Army's Leadership Field Manual.

You might assume that the U.S. Army Leadership Field Manual (FM) is a large and extensive volume of information, when in fact the manual is only 212 pages long. The latest update, Army Doctrine Reference Publication 6-22 (ADRP 6-22), is 198 pages. The Army doesn't produce books in a traditional sense; they have a publication system. This system does not have individual authors, so their publications are collaborative works over time. Examples of Army publications are:

ADP   Army Doctrine Publications
ADRP   Army Doctrine Reference Publications
TM   Technical Manuals
TLP   Troop Leadership Procedures
STP   Soldier Training Publications
FM   Field Manuals

Currently, the Army titles its leadership publications as ADP or ADRP. However, I have titled this book a Field Manual because I hope that you will take this book into your career field. It is also my hope that you will make this FM a permanent part of your leadership collection, and that you reference it often. You may also find it useful as a training tool for others.

• • •

While the Army's Leadership Field Manual is a superior training tool, it makes an assumption that we cannot make with this Student Leadership Manual—it assumes that you are in the Army, and it assumes that you have been through basic training, the very first step in the process of becoming an Army leader.

For the purposes of understanding how the Army's leadership method applies to you, I have created the acronym **B.A.S.I.C.,** and in the following pages I will 'unpack' each of these elements.

FRED GROOMS

B. Behavior
A. Attitude
S. Skills
I. Integrity
C. Choices

Part One

Leadership

1-1. It's important that you understand why there is so much emphasis placed upon leadership and developing leadership potential. Leadership is inevitable; leadership has a way of finding you, so you might as well be prepared. And as a society we are faced with an upcoming *leadership gap*.

The Leadership Gap

1-2. The leadership gap is the gap between those who are currently in leadership positions and those who will be leading in the future. That means *you*. You and your peers will be filling that gap. It is estimated that by the year 2030, nearly half of those currently employed in the U.S. will have retired, and that will leave a *big gap* in experienced leaders. This is going to give you a lot of opportunities to lead at a young age, more than at any other time in history. However, society is concerned about whether your generation is up to the task of leading us in the future. Personally, I'm not concerned; I've seen the amazing things students like you can accomplish when given the opportunity. You *are* up to the challenge.

The Call to Leadership

1-3. You will have both a personal and professional call to leadership. As I have already stated, leadership is inevitable. You will be leading your peer group, team, tribe, work mates, friends, family....Every group, job or organization of which you will be a member has some form of leadership requirement. As you progress in your career, you will be leading others. Many of you are already leading others in official or unofficial roles.

Someone is Watching

If you have a younger brother or sister, let me assure you right now that you are leading them. That's right; younger siblings look up to and follow their big brothers and sisters. If you think about that, it's a lot of responsibility. So ask yourself, where are you leading them? What examples are you setting for them to follow? Can you take a more active role?

Perhaps you're on a sports team or in a student organization at your school. If so, you have others that will follow your lead. Most people are willing followers; they prefer to allow others to take charge and lead. Following comes naturally to us whereas leadership takes work.—*Illustration 1*

1-4. We need you to step up now and take on the responsibilities of young leaders. The sooner you invest in being a leader, the better leader you will become.

Leadership Is a Skill

1-5. The good news for each of us is that leadership is a skill. Skills can be taught, learned and invested in. Over time, as you invest in the skill of leadership, you can move towards mastering this skill. Once you begin to master the skill of leadership, you become highly valuable. When you become highly valuable, you become highly sought after. When you are highly sought after, you have more control over your future. Who doesn't want more control over their future? So it is vital that you start developing the skill of leadership today rather than tomorrow.

Leadership Defined

1-6. Leadership is the art and science of influencing others. It is the means by which you get people to accomplish a task or mission. Leadership is not simple management of personnel and supplies. The military often overlaps the terms leader and command/commander. A military commander is expected to inspire the willingness, confidence, respect and loyalty of those in their command so together they can effectively accomplish any job, task or mission.

1-7. As a student, it becomes your responsibility to develop your ability to influence others. You must learn that leadership takes personal responsibility and accountability, and that it takes personal and moral courage. As a leader, you open yourself to criticism, conflict, and questioning. People will push back at your leadership and criticize you personally. They will question every decision you make.

Everybody Leads

I once had a student tell me he was not going to lead or follow anyone; he was going to be his own boss and work on his own. So I asked him what he was going to do to make a living. He shared an idea that he had for an online gaming product that he was developing, and he insisted that he didn't need anyone's help. It sounded like a great idea, and I asked him if he would let me invest $50,000 in his product; but I added that he would have to allow me to share his idea with a friend of mine that works for a major gaming company, and that he would have to show him and others how to use the product. He immediately said yes; and I pointed out that he would then be accepting help, and that he would be both leading and following someone. He was not very happy with me, but leadership is inevitable and everybody follows somebody.—*Illustration 2*

Everybody Follows Somebody

1-8. For the most part, you get to choose the leaders you will follow. That is, if you choose to be an active participant in the process. Too many people just don't get this. Because everyone is following someone, you should be selecting the leaders you want to follow. If you don't, I guarantee that someone will choose *for* you. As a leader, your goal should be to establish the leadership/followership rapport.

Leadership Equals Followership

1.9. I'm not sure when I first heard someone use the term followership, but it helps us understand what it means to truly lead others. Becoming a quality leader means you are equal parts leader and follower. Everybody follows somebody. It is true in the military and it is true in life. With all the emphasis placed on leadership in the Army, it is important to understand that every soldier is also a subordinate or follower. Everyone answers to someone, from the newest private to the highest ranking general officer.

1-10. Being a leader and a follower are unquestionably linked; one does not exist without the other. A leader must have subordinates who are willing to follow him. As a follower you have two choices. You can blindly follow those appointed above you, doing just what you are told to do, when and how you are told to do it. Or, you can choose to become an active participant in the actions of the leader, fully participating in accomplishing the mission or goal, and entering into a followership relationship. If you do the latter, you become part of the leadership process.

The Leadership Process

1-11. Leadership development is a process. There are some individuals who could be described as "natural born leaders." However, there are very few people that have a natural tendency for leadership; the vast majority of us will have to invest in the process—and you are never too young to begin.

1-12. The Army Field Manual (FM) on leadership sets up the leadership process in a "framework." The core of this framework is: *BE, KNOW, DO*. As noted in the Army's FM, paragraph 1-21, a leader's character and competence is the 'BE'; the skills of the leader is the 'KNOW'; and the leader taking action is the 'DO'.

1-13. While the Army's Leadership FM is a superior training tool, it makes an assumption that we in civilian life cannot make; it assumes that you are in the Army. And it assumes that you have been through basic training, the very first step in the process of becoming an Army leader.

1-14. Basic training takes a civilian like you and teaches them the very first steps needed to become a soldier. You learn what it means to be part of a unit. You are taught skills that every soldier must have in order to work and survive as a soldier. Basic training is both a mentally and physically challenging environment. In Basic, you are purposely stressed so that you begin to identify how you will best handle the rigorous requirements of being a solider. You are also given your first opportunity to be in command or lead.

1-15. In this manual, I have taken the foundational elements found in Basic training and the military leadership model and created the acronym B.A.S.I.C. The acronym B.A.S.I.C. is about teaching you how to apply the fundamental elements of Army Basic training to your leadership skills. What is cool about this is that you don't actually have to *go* to the Army Basic training to learn these lessons.

This acronym will assist you as we progress through the training in this FM.

B. Behavior

A. Attitude

S. Skills

I. Integrity

C. Choices

> *"My own definition of leadership is this: The capacity and the will to rally men and women to a common purpose and the character which inspires confidence."*
> —General George Patton

Part One

LEADERSHIP
Discussion Questions

1) Define 'Leadership' as you understand it.

_____

_____

2) On a scale of 1 to 5, do you want to be a leader?

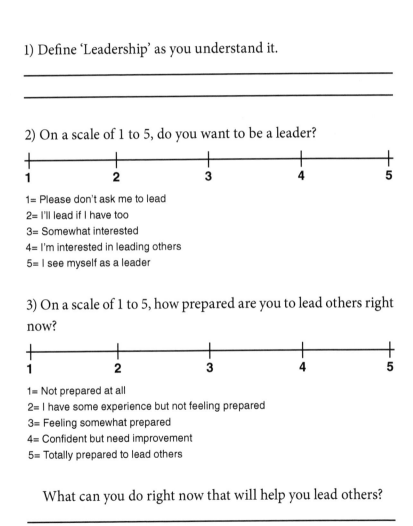

1	2	3	4	5

1= Please don't ask me to lead
2= I'll lead if I have too
3= Somewhat interested
4= I'm interested in leading others
5= I see myself as a leader

3) On a scale of 1 to 5, how prepared are you to lead others right now?

1	2	3	4	5

1= Not prepared at all
2= I have some experience but not feeling prepared
3= Feeling somewhat prepared
4= Confident but need improvement
5= Totally prepared to lead others

What can you do right now that will help you lead others?

_____

_____

4) List examples of how you might better prepare yourself for leadership.

_____

_____

5) Identify 2 or 3 people in your life right now that you would describe as a leader.

_____

_____

6) What makes them a leader?

_____

_____

7) On a scale of 1 to 5 and being totally honest, how easily **are you influenced** by your peers?

```
+----------+----------+----------+----------+
1          2          3          4          5
```

1= I'm not influenced at all by my peers.
2= Sometimes they influence me more than I influence them.
3= They influence me but I also influence them.
4= My peers influence me more then I influence them.
5= I'm influenced by my peers most of the time.

8) Are you being influenced in a positive or negative way? Explain.

_____

_____

_____

_____

9) On a scale of 1 to 5, how easy is it for **you to influence** your peers to follow your leadership?

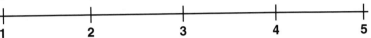

1= They do whatever I say.
2= They follow me most of the time.
3= Sometimes it takes a little effort to get them to follow.
4= It takes more effort than I'd like.
5= Can't get them to do anything I ask.

10) Being totally honest, are you influencing others in a positive or negative way? Explain.

_____

_____

11) The author makes this statement: "Everybody follows somebody. If you don't pick who you follow, someone will pick for you." Do you agree with this statement?

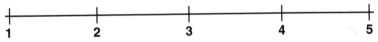

1= Completely disagree.
2= Somewhat disagree.
3= Feeling neutral.
4= Agree somewhat.
5= Completely agree.

Share your thoughts about this statement: "Everybody follows somebody."

_____

_____

_____

Part Two

In Order To Be *In* Command, You Must First Learn To Be *Under* Command

Under Command

2-1. In order to be *in* command you must first learn to be *under* command. This is the most important statement you as a student need to hear. It may also be one of the most misunderstood and difficult leadership concepts to grasp. At a time in your life when you are seeking to gain your independence from others, it sounds as if I am suggesting that you give up the very thing you are desperately seeking…independence.

Independence

2-2. Independence is freedom from the control, support or influence of others. You rely solely on yourself. Sounds good, right? However, complete independence is a luxury seldom attained and seldom truly wanted.

2-3. Why is independence a luxury seldom wanted? Look closely at the definition of independence. It is freedom from the control, support and influence of others; you rely only upon yourself to make choices. It is complete self-sufficiency. Imagine now what life would be like if you were totally and completely independent. You would have no rules and no guidelines on which to base your life. You would have no-one to provide you with support or guidance in any aspect of your life; there would be no-one to support you or influence you in your

15

decision-making; and there would be no sharing of responsibilities. True independence is actually a lonely prospect.

Who Needs Independence?

You might think that true independence actually sounds great—not having anyone to tell you what to do, or who to hang out with, or what you can and cannot do with your free time.

You might even have a friend who seems to have this kind of freedom—no parents or teachers bugging him or her. And you may think they are lucky. However, I can pretty much guarantee that if you asked them, they would trade their "independence" for people in their lives who care about them and support them. Being under the command of others provides us with the structure and support we need in life. It provides us with safety to expand our experiences, learn from mistakes and rebound from poor choices.—*Illustration 3*

2-4. We all start out being completely dependent on others for our every need; we can do nothing on our own. As we get older, we naturally depend less upon others for our basic needs. We learn to dress ourselves, feed ourselves and take care of our personal needs. As we demonstrate our ability to control specific areas of our lives, we move towards greater independence. We then seek to gain greater independent control of *all* areas of our lives. Expressing our personal independence reaches a highpoint when we are teenagers and young adults. This is likely where *you* are right now, wanting greater independent control of your life.

2-5. At this level of independence you begin to make choices for yourself. You are given the opportunity to make "adult choices." You are able to experiment with your personal likes and dislikes. You choose your friends and how you spend your free time. You are making choices about your education, faith, and finances that will affect your future. With each good or bad choice you make, you are gaining experience, and that is a good thing. Hopefully, as you gain experience, you are gaining wisdom. It is this wisdom that guides you to understand and seek *interdependence*.

2-6. Interdependence is the point at which individuals adjust their personal independence in order to support each other. You find mutual support in your strengths and weaknesses. This is the point where your independence and the independence of others come together to achieve the goals that you and they aspire to. You learn to choose to come *under command* and to be *in command*; you are interdependent.

Destroying Your Life

Independence for me was about money. The more money I could make, the more independent I felt. When I was in high school I spent most of my time working a full time job; school wasn't important to me. I had a great job and I was making a lot of money. I bought my own car and took care of it. No one told me what I could or could not wear because I bought my own clothes. Because I made my own money, I never needed to ask my parents for money, and I could spend my money on whatever my heart desired.

I was independent, my own man; and no one was telling me what to do with my life. I had it made—or so I thought.

When I was a junior in high school, I came home from work and my father was waiting for me in the kitchen. He was not happy. He was holding a crumpled piece of paper in his hand. He looked at me and proclaimed, "Son, you're destroying your future!"

I thought to myself, "What on earth could my father be holding in his hand that showed I was destroying my future?" So I asked him what he was holding.

"I have your interim grade report. If you keep going like you are right now, you are going to fail high school, and if you fail out you will get out!"

My father doesn't say stuff he doesn't mean, and what he meant was that I'd have to move out of his house. I actually thought my father was exaggerating about destroying my life, but then he started to break down the numbers with me and I could see that he was right.

School and I never got along; I was never a good student. I'm dyslexic, and that meant that I had a lot of trouble learning to read and write; which put me behind in school from an early age and I never caught up. At a time when everyone else seemed to be doing great in school, I was that kid who just couldn't keep up and who was always in trouble.

As I got into middle and high school, I also had a "don't give a care" attitude. I wasn't any good at school so I was going to give it as little effort as possible. All I wanted from school was to get out of school.

My first thought when my father pointed out that I was going to fail high school was: "Okay, so let me just drop out of school and work." It seemed reasonable to me. Then my father ran the financial numbers with me. It became obvious that as long as I was living with my parents, I was making good money, but as soon as I was independent of them, my well-paying job wasn't looking so good. Bills add up quickly when you're living alone.

But I *felt* independent. I was making my own money and my own choices. What I failed to realize was that the choices I was making were actually limiting my future independence. If I kept going like I was, it was a virtual guarantee that I would be limiting my future potential if not destroying it all together.

So at a time when I thought that all I wanted was to be fully independent, what I really needed was to learn to come 'under command.' I had to come under the command of the educational system and allow it to help me into the future. I had to come under the command of my teachers and parents that knew more about stuff then I did.

When I came under command, I actually expanded my future opportunities rather than limiting them. I graduated high school at the bottom of my class, but I graduated. Then I literally talked my way into a military university. Once there, I graduated in the top third of my class, earned a commission in the U.S. Army, and the rest is history.—*Illustration 4*

2-7. Learning to come under command is something that *all* successful leaders must do, and it can be challenging. Placing yourself under someone's command is not always easy, especially when you are young and you are just starting to feel yourself gaining some independence. But being under command is not about surrendering your independence; it is about gaining your *future* independence.

2-8. One of the most important aspects of the military model of leadership is that *every* soldier, no matter their rank, is both a leader and a subordinate at the same time. They are both in command and under command, and this creates a mutual respect for each other. No leader is better than the subordinates he or she is leading. This is definitely true as a young officer. You will be in command of soldiers that are old enough to be your parent, and they will have much more experience than you. Yet, they will voluntarily come under your command and follow your example and your leadership.

2-9. A new recruit in the Army takes their first step towards becoming a leader by coming under the command of their instructor as they enter Basic military training.

2.10. So now it's time for you to enter into your own B.A.S.I.C. leadership training.

"Accept the challenge so that you feel the exhilaration of victory."
—General George Patton

In Order to Be in Command You Must First Learn to Be Under Command

1) How independent are you right now?

```
+-------------+-------------+-------------+-------------+
1             2             3             4             5
```

1= Completely dependent on others.
2= I have some independence but still get significant support.
3= I'm working towards greater independence.
4= I'm more independent than most of my peers.
5= Totally independent.

2) Describe what being independent looks like for you.

_____

_____

3) Explain what it means to be: dependent, independent and interdependent.

Dependent: _____

Independent: _____

Interdependent: _____

4) Explain in your own words what you think the author means by: "In order to be in command you must first learn to come under command."

_____

_____

_____

5) The author makes this statement: "You must learn to come under command before you can be in command." Do you feel like he is asking you to give up your independence?

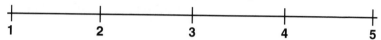

1= Completely feel like he is asking me to give up my independence.
2= He is, but he might be right.
3= Feeling neutral.
4= To some extent he is, but not totally.
5= No, I don't think he is asking me to give up my independence.

Explain why you feel the way you do about question #5.

_____

_____

_____

6) The author says that leadership is inevitable and unavoidable for everyone. Do you believe he is right?

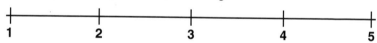

1= Nope, never leading anyone.
2= Hoping leadership doesn't find me.
3= I'll lead if I have to.
4= Looking forward to leading others.
5= Leadership is my destiny.

Part Three: Section 1

B.A.S.I.C. Student Leadership
BEHAVIOR

Standards of Behavior

3-1-1. When you enter the military, you are expected to adjust your behavior so as to come under command and conform to the Army standards of behavior. You will be taught to walk differently, stand differently, and talk differently. You will be expected to assimilate into a wildly diverse culture and work alongside a wide range of people. You will be held accountable for your behavior both on and off duty. Civilian organizations do not require such a drastic transition, but the lessons we teach in the Army are extremely valuable not just for those who serve in the military, but for you as well.

Uniform of the Day

3-1-2. The Army is full of formality, new terminology and sights and sounds, and plenty of dos and don'ts; it is definitely a shock to a new recruit. Everything around them is new and different, and the Army expects them to adapt quickly. Within minutes a new recruit is expected to start walking and talking differently than when they got off the bus. It is expected of them to immediately come under a new command authority, a new form of leadership.

3-1-3. A formal part of transitioning to come under the command of the military for both men and women is a change of clothing. Everyone is placed in a new uniform, their duty uniform. This is the same uniform that every soldier wears, and there is nothing special about anyone's uniform; what makes the uniform special is the individual wearing it. When you are wearing the uniform of a soldier, you are expected to behave like a solider.

3-1-4. The same is true in civilian life as well. When you take your first "real" job you are sure to find it somewhat of a shock. Your employer is going to expect you to learn their industry terminology, dress appropriately based on their business model, and quickly adjust to their behavioral standards.

Modify Your Behavior—The Disney Way

The military is not alone when it comes to asking its members to modify their behavior and even their appearance. Many civilian corporations have very specific dress codes and standards of behavior that they expect their employees to follow.

Perhaps one of the best civilian examples comes from Disney. Disney has a very strict code of conduct and they require their employees to conform to this code both on-duty and off-duty. Disney requirements include a very specific dress code; every employee is required to wear a costume or uniform, and they are not allowed to alter that it in any way. According to disneycareers. com, "The Disney look is a classic look that is clean, natural, polished and professional, and avoids 'cutting edge' trends or extreme styles. It is designed with our costumed and non-costumed cast members in mind. Our themed costumed cast members are a critical part of enhancing the experience of our Disney show, and our non-costumed cast members also play an important role as representatives of the Disney brand. Regardless of the position you hold with us, when you take pride in your appearance, you become a role model for those around you, and you convey the attitude of excellence that has become synonymous with the Disney name."

Disney will not allow any body alterations and that includes any visible tattoo. Most uniforms are short sleeved or have a short-sleeved version. You can't have your tongue pierced, or multiple ear piercings, or ear gages. Nor can you have 'hidden' piercing that can been seen through your uniform.

Disney also has a strict standard for both men and woman on how employees keep their hair. Men must shave every day, and if they have facial hair it must be fully grown in and meet a high standard of grooming. A five-day shadow look is out of the question.

For women, "if makeup is worn, it should be applied in a blended manner and in appropriate, neutral colors." Disney even has a requirement for the length of your fingernails, and if painted, they must be an approved neutral color.

You can forget checking your phone while 'on stage,' and photos while on stage and backstage are prohibited. Disney also has policies that restrict your usage of social media, and you're not allowed to post on social media about your time on stage. If you're portraying a Disney character, such as a princess, your restrictions are even greater than those of a regular cast member.

Disney expects that every employee will pick up any trash they come across. They even have a specific way they want you to pick up the trash; it's called the 'trash scoop.'

The bottom line is that if you wish to be an employee of Disney, you will have to come under the command of the industry requirements. You will have to learn their methods and their terminology, dress appropriately, and learn the trash scoop.—*Illustration 5*

3-1-5. Most high schools and many middle schools have one or more Career and Technology Student Organizations (CTSOs). Each of these organizations has a dress code and requires specific formal dress for meetings. It is their duty uniform. The reason is simple: you are representing everything that the group stands for. When you are a member, they expect you to adjust your behavior and come under command in such a way that reflects their core principles and values. When you are wearing their coat with their logo on it, they have very specific expectations of you; and if you violate those expectations, there are consequences. When you wear the uniform of your organization, you are representing something greater than yourself.

3-1-6. As a leader you are always representing someone. The person whom you are representing expects you to behave in a particular manner. This will include what you say and the tone in which you say it. You are always setting an example, good or bad, on or off duty.

3-1-7. "Everyone loves a man [woman] dressed in uniform." You may have heard this saying before. I think the saying is totally accurate, and the uniform does not have to be a military uniform. But why do we love someone in uniform? The uniform makes them look and feel important and it is something they have earned. When soldiers wear their dress uniforms for the first time it is an amazing sight. They walk tall and stand proud. It is fun to watch them because they cannot stop looking at themselves in the mirror.

3-1-8. Most jobs have a uniform or dress code of some sort, and you need to get used to this fact. Even if you're an entrepreneur, you are going to be representing your product or brand and your customers will expect you to look the part. So if you work for a top accounting firm, they will most certainly expect you to dress in quality business attire. If you own a surf shop and make surf boards, it's fine for you to wear your flip flops, old Van's t-shirt and board shorts, and be covered in board dust. However, if you have a meeting with a large sports distributor who wants to put your surf boards in all of their stores, you'd better rethink your wardrobe choice for the meeting. You don't have to put on a suit and tie, as that would not fit your brand. You should go to the meeting in a brand new pair of Van's shoes, pressed pants, and your company logo t-shirt. Comb the dust out of your hair and find a jacket. You are no longer just a surf shop owner. You will be representing the sports distributor and they will have different expectations.

Uniform of the Day

The local community college trains students to enter into a wide range of medical careers, and there is a dress code for every student who is working in a hospital or health care facility.

Every student, male or female, is required to wear a white medical uniform and white shoes. These are not hospital scrubs. They wear a pressed uniform with the school logo over one breast pocket and their name tag over the other pocket. This uniform looks sharp, as do the students in them. You definitely notice them.

I once had the opportunity to speak to some of the students, and I asked them how they felt about their uniform. They were in agreement that at first they did not like the idea of the undeviating white uniform. However, once they put it on and began working in the hospital environment, something came to their attention: people noticed them and commented on how professional they looked. I asked them if the uniform made a difference in how they did their jobs; and again, the students were in agreement. They felt that the uniform gained them respect which made doing their jobs easier. It's amazing what happens when you come under command. You gain respect.—*Illustration 6*

Military/Personal Bearing

3-1-9. I like to say that it is your poise, presence and posture that gets you initial respect; it is about how you carry yourself.

The image you project matters. Have you ever seen someone walk into a room and command respect? Their very presence makes you stop and take notice. Believe it or not, this is a leadership skill you can develop. You have to have a high level of confidence in yourself and your ability. When you are well dressed, prepared for anything, and highly skilled, it shows. Others will take notice.

The F-Bomb

One evening at a large youth conference where I had been a speaker, the elevators in the main lobby were not stopping. The conference had just let out and there was a large crowd of students gathering at the main elevators. As the crowd grew, so did the frustration with the wait.

Then a young man walked up to the back of the crowd and asked in a loud voice if there was a problem. The crowd parted as this student made his way to the elevator doors. He must be someone important, I thought. I noticed that he was wearing his organizational dress coat and a name tag that said "President." This young man obviously commanded respect from the other students. He even offered an explanation as to why the elevators were not stopping.

"The elevators are full from the lower floors so they will not stop," he said. "This happens all the time." A reasonable explanation, I thought, and the crowd seemed to agree. Then this young man, having the attention of the crowd, started asking the other students questions about the event. Good job, I thought to myself, he is distracting the students from their long wait.

But then it happened. As he continued to hold the crowd's attention, he started making jokes. At first his comments were somewhat funny but they then became crude. The more the students laughed, the cruder the jokes became, and by this time he had several of his friends joining in. Everyone was laughing until he dropped the f-bomb, not once, but several times in a row. At this point, he still had not taken notice of me standing directly behind him.

After he had dropped the f-bomb several times, the crowd of students hushed. He immediately noticed the change in the mood, and that every student was no longer looking at him but past him. He turned around to see why and he noticed me standing behind him.

As if on cue, all the elevators starting opening and the students poured into the empty elevators. This young man's friends were the first to abandon him; they practically dove into the open elevators. He found himself standing there alone looking at me. I turned and got into an open elevator, leaving him in the lobby.

The next morning as I was prepping for a breakout session, the young man came in. He introduced himself and offered me an apology. I respected him for that; however, the people he owed an apology to were not in the room. This young man now had a leadership problem; his behavior had damaged his ability to lead and he knew it.—*Illustration 7*

3-1-10. As a leader you have to maintain control of your emotions. You have to have self-control because this affects your interactions with others. You have probably dealt with someone who is highly emotional; perhaps someone who allows himself or herself to become easily angered or frustrated, or who gets discouraged or upset easily. These people are emotional time bombs and no one wants their leaders to be this way. If someone has a tendency to be this way, they are difficult to predict, and their team is less likely to come to them in a time of need or crisis. Their emotional state cannot be trusted.

3-1-11. Effective leaders keep their emotions in balance. They don't let their moods affect their leadership. They display the right emotions at the right time. Do not think you have to be emotionless. You have to draw upon your emotions to let your team know you understand their perspective in any situation. However, there are times where you have to be the steadiest and most levelheaded person on the team; and of course this is especially true in times of stress. Your team will feed off your emotions. If you are out of control, your subordinate team members may follow suit. Basically, you have to display the emotions you want your subordinates to display. *(See 3-2-25 for more.)*

3-1-12. This is where some military leaders miss the mark. As an Army Officer, you tend to believe that you are to "show no fear," when in reality you are as afraid as the next soldier. As a leader, it is perfectly acceptable to be mad, sad, afraid, or joyfully happy. The key is to acknowledge your emotions with your team and express them appropriately, and to not let one emotion control your entire attitude. As a student leader you must learn to balance your emotions.

"Do more than what is required of you."
—General George Patton

Part Three, Section 1

BEHAVIOR
Discussion Questions

1) Have you ever had a leadership position or job or situation where you were required to dress in a specific "duty" uniform? (Perhaps it was a school dress code.)

Yes or No

2) Describe how you initially felt when you first dressed in the required uniform.

_____

_____

3) Do you think it made a difference in your performance? Explain why or why not.

_____

_____

4) How do you feel about the fact that you will be required to modify your behavior to fit the standards and culture of your work environment?

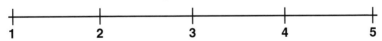

| 1 | 2 | 3 | 4 | 5 |

1= Totally ticked.
2= Wish I had more control.
3= Feeling neutral.
4= I guess it's okay.
5= Totally fine with it.

Discuss your answer:

_____

_____

5) Do you believe someone can control a room based simply on their personal presence or behavior?

```
+---------+---------+---------+---------+
1         2         3         4         5
```

1= No way, not possible to control a room with just your presence.
2= Perhaps there are a few people who can control a room.
3= Feeling neutral.
4= With effort most people can learn to control a room.
5= Anyone can control a room with their presence.

Discuss your answer:

_____

_____

6) Do you agree that controlling your behavior is a skill you can develop?
Yes or No.

7) What do you think it would require to develop a personal presence as a skill? Discuss your answer:

_____

_____

_____

_____

_____

8) Reread Illustration #7 "The F-Bomb." Then write down / discuss what leadership mistakes this student made and what you think he should do to fix them.

_____

_____

_____

_____

9) How important is it for you as a leader to control your emotions?

```
+------+------+------+------+
1      2      3      4      5
```

1= Not important at all.
2= Somewhat important.
3= Important.
4= Very important.
5= It's necessary to maintain complete control all the time.

Discuss your answer:

_____

_____

10) Describe how as a leader you might show your team how you are feeling while at the same time maintaining control of your emotions?

_____

_____

_____

_____

_____

Part Three: Section 2

B.A.S.I.C. Student Leadership ATTITUDE

Attitude vs. Happiness

3-2-13. The US Army Leadership model puts a significant amount of importance on a soldier's *attitude*. Not once does it mention a soldier's happiness. As an Army leader you are responsible for your unit's morale, but morale is not about whether your subordinates are happy. Morale is about confidence, drive, and optimism.

Happiness

3-2-14. Our society places a lot of importance on personal happiness. We want to be happy and we want others around us to be happy. This is true on a different level for students. Youth not only want to be happy; they *expect* others to make sure they are happy. But this is not reality. Consequently, young leaders make the mistake of believing it is their responsibility to make those they are leading happy. However, as a leader, your job is to accomplish the goals, tasks, or objectives set for you by the leadership above you; it is not to make people happy.

3-2-15. Science tells us that an individual's happiness is subjective. No one can judge someone else's happiness but them. Essentially, being happy is about having a positive attitude or a general feeling of "happiness" in the present, and a positive outlook for the future. Therefore, as a leader, you cannot be responsible for your individual team members' happiness. You cannot make others happy, but you can affect their attitude.

Attitude

3-2-16. Attitude is about will, grit, tenacity, perseverance, and focus. You may find it surprising that a person's attitude towards success is actually an equal or better predictor of future success than IQ and GPA. Employers look for individuals who can demonstrate that they have the will and grit to stick to projects until completion. They need people who can persevere in the long term as the work environment changes rapidly. Like the Army, civilian employers need individuals who can get the job done no matter what.

3-2-17. Your attitude drives how you see success. As a leader, if you want to affect the happiness of individuals in your organization, team, or tribe, think about influencing their overall attitude and mood. You do this by setting the example. How you as the leader respond in any given situation sets the tone for the entire organization.

3-2-18. Your attitude will affect the attitude of others. If you approach every job with an attitude of success, your team will follow your example. The opposite is true as well. If you have a poor attitude, so will your team. First and foremost a leader leads by example.

Leadership Attitude

Imagine that you are tasked with planning a leadership training event for 200 students who will be coming from all over your state.

You have made reservations for meeting rooms and lodging at a local conference center and hotel. The contracts are signed and everything is ready to go. Several times in recent weeks you have spoken with an employee of the conference center and they have assured you that everything has been taken care of.

The day before the event you arrive at the conference center with your team of 10 students only to find out that there is a major problem. In fact, the conference center did not schedule any meeting rooms for your event, and all the meeting rooms are full. And it gets worse. They do not have any hotel rooms booked either. A conference center employee completely dropped the ball. None of this is your *fault*, but it is still your *responsibility*. What are you going to do?

This is a nightmare situation and it actually happened to a group I was speaking for. The leader of the group had a major problem on her hands. Fortunately, after a brief moment of panic, she regained her composure and immediately started working on a solution. The hotel was able to work out alternate meeting spaces and they booked rooms in the hotel next door. By the time everyone else arrived, they had a plan in place.

So this is an example where the entire event was thrown into question. The leadership team of adults and students had to work extremely diligently to make this event happen. They could easily have allowed their attitude in this unexpected situation to destroy the entire event.

However, the leadership team got together and made sure to maintain a positive attitude. They knew how important their attitude would be to the success of the event. Everyone was inconvenienced in some way, and if the leadership team had spent time complaining and griping, so would everyone else. They had to work extra hard to maintain a positive attitude, and by doing so they rescued the situation and managed to have a hugely successful event.—*Illustration 8*

Persevere with Positivity

3-2-19. In any organization, the leadership has to be able to prevail in adverse situations. The student leaders in *Illustration 8* could have chosen to call off their event, but they chose to persevere and maintain a positive attitude. We all experience situations in our lives when it would be easier to just give up and quit rather than finish what we have started. It is at these times that we need to find the inner strength to press on and finish what we have begun.

3-2-20. When life gets difficult, you can lie down, give in, and quit. You can also stand up, stay strong, get focused, and persevere. As a quality leader there will be times when you have to summon the will to continue. You need to find the will to keep going when you are exhausted, or afraid of what others might think, or tired of all the extra hours. It takes experience and practice to consistently maintain an attitude of success. When you are a leader, others will be watching how you deal with difficult situations.

3-2-21. Perseverance takes self-discipline. Self-discipline is not only an attitude; it is a skill. A self-disciplined attitude means you are willing to take care of business the right way all the time. As a leader, it is your job to set the example in the area of self-discipline. If you expect others to come under your command, you must set the example of being under command yourself. If there are rules to follow, you should set an example by following them. No one should be "above the law" and that includes you as a leader. Why would you expect your team to put in long hours if you are not putting in the same hours or more? If you are going to expect your team members to arrive early and stay late, you should be the first to arrive and the last to leave. When things get out of control, and they will at times, you have to be self-disciplined enough to take command of the situation and make levelheaded choices. Stay cool and lead by example.

Perseverance

Becoming an Army Ranger is one of the most difficult tasks a soldier can take on. Ranger school is designed to be physically challenging and mentally fierce, and it consists of three phases lasting 60 days. Less than half of the soldiers who enter the training graduate, and a third have to repeat at least one phase.*

Rangers will tell you the greatest challenges you will face in Ranger School are mental. In order to achieve success, you must have command over your attitude. When you are physically exhausted, wet, cold, and hungry, you have to summon an attitude of success. When you want to give up the most is when you must decide that you can do what you never thought possible. It is essential that you mentally push yourself beyond what you thought you could do physically. You look to your team members for support and encouragement; you know you are not alone. You know that together you can accomplish more than you could ever hope to achieve alone.

Some of the most difficult things I have accomplished in my life have come as a direct result of the training I received in the Army. There is no substitute for being in an environment that pushes you mentally and physically beyond what you ever thought you could endure.

I once found myself lying completely still for hours in the direct summer sun with temperatures reaching 120 degrees. Doing this takes mental courage. You know that if you move, the enemy is so close that they will see you. If they see you, they will attack. If they attack, you and your team will be done for. So you will yourself to lie there without moving. As painful as it is, you lie there motionless until it is safe to do otherwise.

When you are so mentally exhausted you can barely think, yet you can find some way to laugh at the craziness of your situation, you know you have mastered your attitude and you can handle whatever comes next.—*Illustration 9*

*Statistics are from the U.S. Army Maneuver Center of Excellence website

Morale

3-2-22. As a student leader, it is your responsibility to create an atmosphere of confidence and optimism. An organization that is fueled with a high degree of confidence is an organization that can accomplish seemingly impossible jobs. You give your subordinates confidence by making sure they are trained well to do their jobs and by allowing them the freedom to prove it. You give individuals room to make mistakes, and you create a system that allows people to learn from their mistakes. Treat everyone with respect and you will create the kind of morale that results in a loyal, cohesive team.

3-2-23. Optimism is knowing you can accomplish anything. It comes from having confidence in yourself and your team, and knowing that what you are doing matters in some way. Again, as a leader, you set the example for your organization and your team. No one wants their leader to be a "glass is half-empty" guy. You have to be the one that sees the glass as half-full.

3-2-24. Too many people in leadership positions believe that as the leader they are not allowed to have fun. They believe that their subordinates need to see them as always being tough and always being mission focused. Who wants to work for someone that can't ever take a break? Life should be fun, and I think it is most often funny if you let it be. You should find ways to allow your crew to blow off steam. Great leaders create opportunities for their teams to have fun together; it is one of the best ways to create personal bonds that positively affect morale. You have to give your team time off, and you as the leader must also take time away from work. Without time off, you and your team will "burn out." Burnout can happen to even the best leaders, but you can prevent it by taking necessary time off.

Attitude Is Powerful

3-2-25. Have you ever been with someone whose mood is completely unpredictable moment to moment? They are happy one minute and upset or annoyed or depressed the next. People like this are hard to be around because they are so unpredictable. Your attitude is a powerful tool that will affect your success and failure. So why do we give the power of our attitude away so easily?

3-2-26. What I mean by giving the power of your attitude away is this: when you allow someone else to make you angry over something that really does not matter, you give the power of your attitude away. If you hold a grudge against someone for something they did weeks ago or even years ago, you give the power of your attitude away. If there is that one person on your team that you just do not like and you allow them to make your job difficult, you are giving the power of your attitude away. If you are assigned a seemingly impossible task and you immediately assume you cannot make it happen, you give the power of your attitude away.

3-2-27. Most importantly, if you allow other people's negative opinion of you to affect your attitude, you give them power over you. If you let other people control how you feel about yourself, you allow them to define your success and your self-worth. *You get to define the power of your attitude, not others.*

Attitude Shift

You are hanging out with four of your friends listening to music. Everyone is having a great time laughing about their day, talking about the weekend coming up, and singing along with the newest hits on the radio. The volume is up way too loud but who cares, you're having a great time. Then all of a sudden, your friend sitting in the front passenger seat of the car starts crying for no apparent reason at all. Only moments earlier she was singing out loud and now she is curled up in a ball with big tears running down her face. Everyone else is now dead quiet. You turn down the radio and ask her: "What's up?"

Through her tears and with an unsteady voice, she says, "It's that song...it's the song on the radio." It reminds her of something sad and now she is awash in tears. You try to make it better but no one can console her. Even changing the station doesn't help. Your entire group's attitude is now taken hostage by one girl crying about a song that reminds her of something sad. You're not even sure what it is about the song that is making her sad, but she has killed the mood. One Taylor Swift song is all it takes.

Guys are just as bad, maybe even worse, when it comes to sports. Everybody has a guy friend who is a college football fanatic. They live and die by how their team plays ball on Saturday. If their team loses the game on Saturday, just stay away from them until sometime Tuesday afternoon. By then, they will be focused on how their team could possibly still be in the running for a championship.—*Illustration 10*

3-2-28. There is always someone who is going to be the complainer or pessimist. Do not allow others to control your attitude. Remember, as the organizational leader, your attitude sets the example for others to follow. Maintain an attitude focused on success and so will your team.

A 'Take the Initiative' Attitude

3-2-29. Army leaders are fond of telling their subordinates to 'take the initiative.' The goal is to empower their subordinates to stand up and make a difference for themselves, for the unit and for the overall mission. Initiative is the ability to be a self-starter. As a young student leader, one of the best ways to advance your opportunities as a leader is to demonstrate to your superior that you can act correctly or make good decisions when there are no clear instructions. When you are faced with a situation that has changed, you step up and create a new plan. The need for someone to take the initiative motivates a leader to seek out a solution when a plan falls apart. You figure out what needs to get done and you make a decision to get things done, rather than sit around wishing someone would do something. As we say in the Army, you must take the initiative to improvise, adapt and overcome your current situation to get the job done.

> *"By perseverance, study, and eternal desire, any man can become great."*
> —General George Patton

Part Three, Section 2

ATTITUDE
Discussion Questions

1) Rate how happy you are right now.

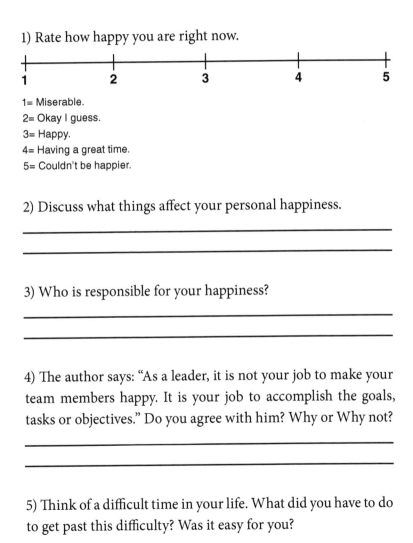

1= Miserable.
2= Okay I guess.
3= Happy.
4= Having a great time.
5= Couldn't be happier.

2) Discuss what things affect your personal happiness.

_____

_____

3) Who is responsible for your happiness?

_____

_____

4) The author says: "As a leader, it is not your job to make your team members happy. It is your job to accomplish the goals, tasks or objectives." Do you agree with him? Why or Why not?

_____

_____

5) Think of a difficult time in your life. What did you have to do to get past this difficulty? Was it easy for you?

_____

_____

6) Describe what you think it means to "persevere with positivity?"

_____

_____

7) Being totally honest, how easily do you allow other people's attitudes to affect your attitude?

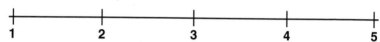

1   2   3   4   5

1= Other people never affect my attitude.
2= On occasion others can affect my attitude.
3= I'm relatively stable with my attitude.
4= More often than not, other people affect my attitude.
5= I'm very easily affected by other people's attitude.

8) Based on Illustration #10, what is your reaction to a Taylor Swift song?

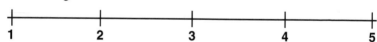

1   2   3   4   5

1= I cry every time I hear a Taylor Swift song.
2= She makes me happy.
3= Feeling neutral.
4= I can't stand Taylor Swift.
5= Who is Taylor Swift?

9) Describe how powerfully you think your attitude affects your current and future success?"

_____

_____

Part Three: Section 3

B.A.S.I.C. Student Leadership
SKILL

Defining Skill

3-3-30. Skill is the actual ability to accomplish a specific task. You are skilled when you can carry out a task to 'near perfection.' Every soldier must master basic skills, such as marching drills, rifle marksmanship, first aid, and map reading, prior to moving on to the other advanced skills. The same is true for any civilian industry. You have to learn the basic skills of your job whether it is accounting, nursing, business marketing, construction, or welding.

3-3-31. Skill is also often defined as knowledge. Knowledge is simply what you have learned or know. You can acquire knowledge through education and/or experience. Knowledge includes basic education, being able to read and write, do math, science, history, and language. You need to have a solid educational foundation in order to learn highly skilled tasks. Skill and knowledge go hand in hand, much like being a leader and a follower.

Expert Professional Skills

3-3-32. Every job, position, and career has very specific skills for that profession. You must learn those basic skills. Once you have mastered the basic skills, you will be expected to move on to more difficult tasks. With each new skill, you gain confidence in your ability. With confidence comes the will and desire to learn more complicated tasks. As you gain confidence you move towards full mastery of a skill. You become an expert.

3-3-33. You *are* an *expert.* I am confident that everyone reading this book is an expert at something right now. You have mastered some skill, something that you can do to near perfection every time you do it. Maybe it is juggling a soccer ball, baking a cake, replacing the brakes in a car, filling out an account balance sheet, or showing a calf at the state fair. I could give examples all day long of what you might be an expert at.

3-3-34. In order to be an expert, all you need is knowledge and skill in a specific area so you can accomplish a task that many other people cannot. Seldom are we willing to give ourselves credit for what we actually know how to do. This is true for students as well as adults. Why? Because we believe that there is always someone better than us. While, that is typically true; there is almost always someone better than you at most things. However, it does not mean you are not an expert too. Do you think there is only one expert on the subject of leadership, finances, surgery, fixing your car, or building a house? Certainly not—there are many experts in every field imaginable.

3-3-35. One of the reasons I like working with the Career Technology Student Organizations (CTSOs) is that they help you develop your expertise early in life. They give students opportunities to experiment in many different areas. They also place a good deal of emphasis on learning leadership skills. Check closely at your school to see which CTSO organizations might be available to you.

Expert Marksmanship

Every soldier must qualify with their service rifle in order to gradu-ate basic training. Many new recruits dread this phase of training. Every soldier carries a weapon, so it is understandable why the Army places so much emphasis on this basic skill.

Rifle marksmanship training takes two weeks. At the end of training, every soldier must meet the minimum standard of hitting 23 out of 40 popup targets. Targets range from 50 meters to 300 meters (3.3 football fields) away. If you can hit 36 or more targets, the Army considers you an expert marksman. Only 1 in 5 individ-uals reach the goal of being an expert marksman.

Does this mean you are sniper qualified? Not even in the movies are you that good. It does mean you have reached a skill level that most soldiers cannot. It qualifies you as an expert in basic rifle marksmanship.—*Illustration 11*

3-3-36. As an officer in an artillery unit, I am not expected to know every little detail of every gun system I might be assigned to lead. However, I am expected to have a working knowledge of each system and have a high degree of confidence in my subor-dinate leaders' ability to be experts on each system. As a leader, you cannot know every specific task of each team member but you need to have a general knowledge of what everyone is doing. In the Army we start everyone off as a leader of a small unit. This allows you to learn what each team member is responsible for. As you rise in the ranks, you take that experi-ence with you, which allows you to be a better leader. You do not get to jump rank.

3-3-37. This is not always the case in the civilian workforce. Leaders jump rank all the time, so you have to work even harder at making sure you know what your subordinate team members are doing. The CEO with 500 or 5000 employees is not going to know what everyone's job is, but they need to have a working knowledge of who does what.

Learn One Teach One

3-3-38. Once you have mastered a task in the military, we do something that is seldom done these days in the civilian workforce. The military *expects* you to teach someone else what you know. If you are the very best at a skill, you will be asked to teach others. No matter your rank, your expertise is valued. Teaching others is a *lost leadership skill*. We tend to only value our own expertise. We think it makes us more valuable if we are the only one who can do something. But in fact, you are more valuable if you can teach others what you know.

Teach Me

In order to lead you, I need to know what you are capable of. As a commander, if I have a new piece of technology or equipment that my soldiers will be using, I need to know how it works. If I have a 19-year-old private who is trained in the new technology, he or she is the expert, not me. I am going to expect this young soldier to teach me what he or she knows. As a leader, I sometimes need to be humble enough to let my followers lead the way.— *Illustration 12*

3-3-39. Every soldier is cross-trained to do someone else's job. At any time, you are at risk of losing a team member. After all, the Army is a dangerous place in wartime. It is a system that is built around attrition; that is, we expect loss through injury or death. So we make sure that each person is trained to do someone else's job. You are not going to be an expert, but you can take care of the basics. We also participate in *training up*. Training up is when you teach your subordinates to take over your job.

3-3-40. Leading in such a manner is one of the best ways you can learn what it means to come under command. As a leader, it is your responsibility to make sure your unit is cross-trained. It is also vital that you are humble enough to train your replacement. This can be a difficult concept in the civilian workplace, where we tend to believe that our value comes from our own expertise. One of the most frustrating things leaders face is the lack of continuity within their workforce. This is a direct result of not cross-training or training your employees on what it takes to do your job. Leaders who lack self-confidence are afraid that teaching someone the inner-workings of their position could be a catalyst for their replacement.

3-3-41. Everyone is replaceable. Weak leaders think their organization cannot do without them, and they believe that there is no reason to be under the command of anyone. Many young leaders are used to being the center of attention; they start to think and feel as if they are indispensable: "Nothing gets done around here without me." It does not matter how senior, or how central, someone is to an organization; they are replaceable. No quality organization is solely built around one individual. Perhaps the dynamics will change if you are gone, but the organization will continue to operate. When someone who is central to the organization leaves or dies, the company must continue on. When Steve Jobs died, Apple continued to develop and sell products, and the company continued to move forward.

Expert Personal Skills

3-3-42. Army schools are much like the advanced education you receive at any college or university. You start with simple skills, later moving to more advanced skills. However, it is well known that there is no substitute for on-the-job training. True leaders recognize that who they are as leaders plays a significant role in how they lead. As a leader, having competence in a specific skill set in your profession is necessary. Yet, you need to develop your *personal* skill set as well. Often we refer to these personal skills as "soft skills." I personally prefer to call them *talents*.

3-3-43. Soft skills, or talents, are those things about you that come naturally. They may include how you naturally deal with others, the way you think about and approach a mission or task, or even how you deal with problems. A great number of talents exist within you, and each of them is very specific. Everyone has a different set of natural talents they rely on. You are talented; you do have soft skills that you use in a unique way. As a young leader, if you want to stand out early, you must begin to identify and invest in these skills.

3-3-44. Your talents are what you do well without any effort. They are your core personality traits. They are the type of things about which your parents might say, "I just don't know where he/she gets it." These talents do not tend to change over time; they are the things about you that remain constant. Your talents empower you. They make it possible for you to move to higher levels of excellence and fulfill your potential. Maybe you are an extrovert. You did not just decide one day to be gregarious and outgoing; it's just the way you are. The same is true for an introvert. However, this is not to say that you are always stuck on either end of the spectrum. It does not mean that as an extrovert you cannot learn to relax and step out of the spot-light. Likewise, an introvert can learn to run meetings and be a public speaker.

Identifying Personal Skills

3-3-45. Identifying your natural talents or personal skills can be difficult at first. As a student, taking your first leadership position can be scary. You are not really sure how you will perform, and I can guarantee that you will first rely upon those things that come naturally to you. How do you start identifying what you are naturally good at? Volunteering for a leadership position may be the best first step. Let your instincts clue you in.

3-3-46. You can also start by asking yourself what you like to do in your free time. Are you someone how likes to be alone or would you prefer to be with a crowd of people? If the power goes out, are you likely to go outside and find something to do, or are you going to grab a candle and a book and start reading? If one of your friends asks a question and no one knows the answer, are you going to grab your smartphone and look up the answer?

3-3-47. Another way to help identify your natural talents is to ask other people what they think you are good at, and then really listen to what they have to say. Sometimes others can see in you what you cannot see in yourself.

3-3-48. Ask yourself what others do that drives you crazy. If someone is a total slob, does that irritate you because you are a total neat freak? You believe everything has its place and every-thing should be in that place. Perhaps one of your friends is spontaneous and you are not. Does that drive you nuts because you are the person that has to have a plan? You are a list-maker and everything has to be done in order. Do you hate speaking in public or do you love it? Do you have a knack for solving problems? Are you a great listener? The answers to each of these questions are indications of what comes naturally to you. Each can lead you to discover your natural talents.*

3-3-49. The Army learned long ago how to discover the natural talents of young leaders: put leaders under stress and see how they react. You can find out a lot about how people will lead by watching what they do under stress. Life is tough, and when things get difficult we are most in tune with what comes naturally to us. So pay close attention to your instincts and how you react to stress, and you will discover some of your greatest soft skills.

Bonus: Find a Mentor

3-3-50. As a young student leader developing your leadership skills, I highly suggest you find a mentor to whom you can come under command. Mentors are people who have the skills, knowledge and experience you want. They have already developed their individual professional and personal expertise, so they can help you shorten your learning curve. If you want to be the very best at something, find someone who you believe is the very best at it and ask them to teach you what they know.

---

*For more information on identifying your natural talents, check out my Amazon bestselling book *Who's in Charge of Bob? Moving from Ordinary to Extraordinary*. This book is all about taking a close look at identifying your natural talents and investing in them to create your own personal strength set.

Expert Leader

In Illustration 4, I mentioned that I am dyslexic. This meant I had a lot of trouble in school. It also meant I had a very low opinion of myself, especially when to me everything that made someone good at something involved their grades, sports, and maybe music. I wasn't good at any of these things. My grades were terrible, and I had to work harder than all my friends in every class just to get by. I was okay at sports, good enough to make the team, but I wasn't a star athlete. As for music, I had no talent at all. When I was young, I thought I had no usable skills or talents, but I was wrong.

Looking back, I know that I had a very narrow view of what it meant to be skilled and talented. I thought to be truly skilled at something you had to be the very best at it, and I knew that there was always someone more skilled and smarter than myself. No way did I ever consider myself to be an expert at anything.

It wasn't until I was a Captain in the Army that I truly felt like I was an expert. My commanding officer sent word to me that I needed to report to his office. Upon arriving, he told me that I had been selected for a very specific mission. I was going to lead a team of 15 soldiers that would develop a plan for retraining another country's military in rifle marksmanship and basic combat training. This would be a huge undertaking.

My commander asked me if I had any questions. I did. My first question was, "Why me, sir?" I looked at the names of the soldiers assigned to the mission and I believed that any one of those men could run the team.

"Captain Grooms, you don't get it, do you?"

"What don't I get, sir?"

"You don't understand that you are one of the very best rifle marksmanship trainers the Army has."

"So is everyone on this list, sir."

"That's true. However, you have other skills that make you the man for this job."

"Thank you, sir."

"Captain Grooms, do you have any other questions?"

"No sir, not at this time."

I walked out of his office, and honestly I felt both a great sense of pride and a great sense of confusion. I still didn't comprehend what he was saying. Sure, I was good at training soldiers, but leading this team seemed to be above my pay-grade, above my skill level.

The next morning, I met with about half of the members of this team. One of those men was Sergeant Jeffcoat, for whom I had high respect. He truly was the best rifle marksmanship trainer I knew. His experience included training snipers and being one himself. He knew way more than I did.

So I asked Sergeant Jeffcoat why he thought I had been selected to command this team.

"Sir, you're an expert."

"At what, Sergeant Jeffcoat?"

"Sir, you are an expert in rifle marksmanship training, and most importantly, you are an expert leader, and there is not a man on this team I would rather be following than you."

That was an incredibly powerful statement to hear. For the first time in my life, I could view myself as an expert. Sergeant Jeffcoat pointed out that I had mastered not only the tangible skills to be an expert trainer in marksmanship but the personal skills to be a leader of men.—*Illustration 13*

"If I do my full duty, the rest will take care of itself."
—General George Patton

SKILL
Discussion Questions

1) The author declares "you are an expert." Do you see yourself right now as an expert at anything?

```
+----------+----------+----------+----------+
1          2          3          4          5
```

1= No way, not me
2= I'm good, but not good enough at anything to be an expert
3= I might be an expert
4= I'm good and working towards being an expert
5= I'm a total expert, better than most

2) Identify three things you can do (skills) that most people you know cannot do. It can be anything at all.

A. _____

B. _____

C. _____

3) Would you consider yourself an expert at any of these three things?

Yes or No

4) If you answered yes, what makes you an expert?

_____

_____

_____

_____

5) If you answered no, why are you not an expert?

_____

_____

6) Now list three of your natural talents (Refer to paragraph 3-3-43). Your natural talents are what you do without any effort.

A. _____

B. _____

C. _____

Think about the following questions to help you answer question #6.

If the power went out, what would you do?

What do you most like to do in your free time?

Ask your friends what they think you're good at.

What do you do that drives others crazy, and can it be a positive?

7) Give an example of how your natural talents might be helpful as a leader.

_____

_____

_____

_____

Part Three: Section 4

B.A.S.I.C. Student Leadership INTEGRITY

Character

3-4-51. It is important to understand that integrity and character are similar and often considered to be synonymous, yet they are not the same. Character describes your ability to do what is right over and over again. You demonstrate character in your actions, and character allows you to act correctly in many different situations.

3-4-52. Good character can be directly related to many of the aspects covered in Section One on behavior. You can actually train character into people. You can teach people to be self-disciplined. You can teach people to be respectful by instructing them to be polite in their speech, saying yes sir and no mam, thank you or no thank you. Showing up on time for work, going to class as expected, getting your homework done, and doing your job at the highest standard possible are demonstrations of your character. Good character is a natural response of consistently acting according to a high standard of behavior in all you do. As a leader, it is the high standards you set for yourself that demonstrate your character.

3-4-53. Every branch of the military, religious organizations, and public schools strive to teach character. How we view and teach character can vary widely from organization to organization. Character education is often about a general set of rules we follow, such as no bullying, being well-mannered, and having civic responsibility.

Integrity

3-4-54. Integrity is actually more important than character. Integrity is built upon your personal core values and morals. It is the deep sense of right and wrong that allows you to consistently act in accordance with your core values. Integrity provides you with the courage to stand for what you know is right.

3-4-55. Having integrity is being able to be truthful and upright all the time despite pressures to do otherwise. Having integrity means acting in accordance with your core values and being true to your character at the same time. As a leader you truly mean and do what you say. "Leaders with integrity do the right thing not because it's convenient or because they have no choice. They choose the right thing because their character permits no less." (The US Army Field Manual 2-32).

Steel Integrity

Engineers often talk about the integrity of steel. Two pieces of steel may look identical from the outside as there is no obvious difference between the two pieces. But an engineer can tell you that when you put the two pieces of steel under stress, they may not be equal. One may break under the weight of the stress. Each piece of steel may not be made out of the same quality of raw material. One piece of steel may have interior flaws. They do not have the same integrity.—*Illustration 14*

Integrity in Leadership

3-4-56. You cannot separate your integrity and character from leadership. As a leader, your life is on display for everyone to see. In the Army, you are accountable for who you are and what you do 24-7. The Army holds their leaders to the highest standards of conduct both on and off duty. As an officer, if you are found guilty of driving under the influence or virtually any other arrest, your career is over. Domestic abuse and adultery are not tolerated and will most often end your career. Lying, cheating, and stealing are also not tolerated at any level. I am not suggesting that every organization is as strict as the Army, but what you do as a leader matters to your organization.

3-4-57. A common mistake young leaders make is believing that they can compartmentalize or separate their on-duty life from their off-duty life. Their mistake is believing that what they do in their free time should not matter to anyone else. This is immature thinking. As a leader you are always on display. If you want your team to follow you, you have to build their confidence in your leadership ability. Their confidence in you is most assuredly going to come from the outward display of your character. If you demonstrate an inability to handle your own personal life, why should you expect anyone to follow your organizational leadership? In order to follow you, your team needs you to be steady and consistent as their leader.

3-4-58. As a leader you are always on display, and that is true today more than at any other time in history. Smartphone technology and social media keeps records of your actions in ways we could never have imagined. Selfies, videos, Snapchat, Facebook, and storage and sharing technology make you and your life available to the masses. "If you do it, someone will capture it." It is difficult to separate your off-duty life and your on-duty life.

Just Because

Immature leaders believe that what they do shouldn't matter to others: "I should be able to do whatever I like with my free time and no one should judge me. Just because I do something crazy, foolish, disrespectful, or shady now and then, doesn't give others the right to judge me." Well, perhaps it does.

"Just because I was mean to that person, sent them mean texts, and gossiped about them with my friends, doesn't make me a mean person."

"Just because I cheated on a test or two, doesn't mean that you shouldn't trust me."

"Just because I like to party, get trashed, fall down, get high, and have fun on the weekends doesn't mean I have bad character."

"Just because I'm chronically late doesn't mean I'm disrespecting you."

Actually, it probably does mean those things. I'm not suggesting that you're not allowed to have fun. I'm suggesting that if you want to be a leader, you have to make your off-duty life reflect the leader you want to be on-duty.—*Illustration 15*

3-4-59. The goal of leadership is to influence others. Mature leaders recognize that they have to inspire confidence in their followers in order to influence their willingness to be lead. You inspire confidence by demonstrating you are a person of integrity and character. You lead by example and earn respect. Once you have gained your followers' confidence, they will follow your lead.

Core Values

3-4-60. If integrity is built based on your core values, what are your core values? Your core values are developed starting at a young age. Your values often start as a direct reflection of your faith, family dynamics, and cultural background. Essentially, your values are what you believe about what is right and wrong. Your values give you a clear sense of what it means to be honest, selfless, loyal, and trustworthy. They provide you with consistency in your actions. Your values are confirmed as you experience their positive results, and they create your personal value system.

3-4-61. As a leader you quickly learn that not everyone has the same values as you. This is even more apparent in the increasingly diverse cultures and backgrounds that are part of our society. You are growing up in a country that no longer has a "common value system," which makes leading a widely diverse team of individuals complicated. The Army is the most diverse organization I have ever been a part of; and the Army deals with the diversity within its ranks by establishing its own core value system. To be a soldier, you must be willing to embrace those values. As a leader in a civilian organization, your team is going to look to you to establish a value system—much like what he Army does for its soldiers. This may sound difficult or even scary. However, it is certainly doable.

Establishing a Value System

3-4-62. Even though we live in a diverse culture, there are common values that we can agree on. Most organizations and employers have rules, regulations, creeds, codes and by-laws that set the standards and policies for the behavior of its members. As the leader, you have to be the one to reinforce the existing value system. You must demonstrate how you expect your team to deal with each other as well as your target audience/customers. It becomes your job to lead by example.

I Solemnly Swear

As an Army officer I swore an oath to uphold the Constitution of the United States, to defend our nation, and to follow the orders of those appointed above me. I took this oath willingly, knowing full well that following this oath could cost me my life. The single most important aspect of this oath was that I knew my leaders and my subordinates took the very same oath. This oath creates a type of bond seldom found outside the military. Because of this oath, I knew that my leaders and subordinates would be willing to put others' needs above their own if necessary.—*Illustration 16*

Establish Selfless Service

3-4-63. Selfless service is leading without the expectation of return or reward. Selfless service is knowing that there are some things that are more important than *you*. History provides us with excellent examples of truly selfless leaders: George Washington, Nelson Mandela, Martin Luther King Jr., Mother Theresa, Mahatma Gandhi, Jesus. These leaders reached the pinnacle of what it means to be a selfless leader.

3-4-64. Selflessly serving others is another example of what I mean when I say, "In order to be in command, you must first come under command." It is not just *you* coming under the command of superiors; it is about serving your followers and actually placing your followers above yourself. The very best leaders are *servant leaders* first.

3-4-65. "If serving is below you, then leading is beyond you." This saying is a powerful reminder that as a leader you should first be a servant, and this means making sure that the basic needs of your followers are being met. The Army considers this the "beans and bullets philosophy." Your soldiers must be well-trained, well-fed, and provided with the necessary supplies to do their jobs. If someone on your team has to do without, it should first be the leader. A simple example is that commanders eat last, not first, in a military setting.

Student Leadership Failure

I was working with a group of adults and students to put on a weekend student event for 3000 students. The student leadership team was primarily responsible for making this event happen, with adult supervision.

The event included a music concert on Saturday evening, and everything was ready for the doors to open at seven o'clock on Saturday evening. Anyone who has been to a student conference or music event that doesn't have assigned seating knows that when the doors open there is always a mad rush to get the front row seats. If you want to be at the front, you have to get in line early. Our event was no exception. Students were in line for over an hour. But something went wrong.

Just before the doors opened, a handful of student leaders went down to the floor of the concert hall and roped off the first six rows. When the doors opened and the rush to the front happened, the first students in line were disappointed that they were unable to get the seats that they had been waiting for because they had been "reserved."

It was well-known that the student leadership had set up a dinner reception for themselves and the band. Each student leader could invite two friends to this reception to meet the band backstage before the concert. The students even had special t-shirts made just for this meet-and-greet session. I was among the few adult leaders that thought this was a bad idea, but we were overruled.

The tension over the reserved section of seats was growing as the arena filled. I suggested to the student leaders that they rethink blocking off this section. However, they felt they had "earned" these seats because of all the work they had done putting on the event. They had indeed worked very hard; however, this was a bad choice.

As the lights went down, the student leaders and their friends came out of the side door of the stage to take their reserved seats. The crowd started to moan. The student president took the microphone on the stage and said with great enthusiasm, "Let's give a hand to the student design team who has worked so hard to put on this event for you."

Close to 3000 students started to "boo!" Instead of being applauded, the leadership team was booed. Their followers felt let down. The audience was focused on the fact that the leaders got the best deal of the night. The leadership had allowed themselves to be more important than those they were there to serve.
—*Illustration 17*

3-4-66. *Servant leadership is becoming another lost leadership skill.* As a young leader, if you can learn the value of servant leadership, your future as a leader is unlimited. It is more likely that you will be personally successful if you help those around you to be successful. "A rising tide floats all boats."

3-4-67. I am not suggesting that you work for free, or that you should not expect to receive benefits for the hard work you put in. If there are no benefits for hard work, then why work at all? However, don't *always* expect a reward or something in return for *everything* you do. The best reward you can receive by serving your subordinates is their *loyalty*.

Establish Loyalty

3-4-68. Leaders can never *demand* loyalty. Loyalty must be earned. Your subordinate team members will give you their loyalty when you make sure they are well taken care of. When you lead in such a way that you set the example in your behavior and your integrity, you earn your team's loyalty. As an Army leader, the soldiers under your command must know you are going to fight *for* them and *with* them. Likewise, when you are under command, you must give your loyalty to the leadership above you.

3-4-69. One of the best ways a young leader can demonstrate their loyalty to their subordinate team members is to never ask your subordinates to do what you as their leader have not been trained to do, have not already done, or are not willing to do with them. No one wants to follow someone they know is not willing to do the very things they are asking their team to do. It does not matter whether you are asking them to dig a ditch, take out the trash, build a rocket ship, or fight a battle. You have to be right there with them. If you ask your team to arrive at an event early and stay late, you must do the same. Their respect for you relies on your mutual effort. If they do not respect you, they will not be loyal to you.

3-4-70. You also establish loyalty by setting high standards for each member of the team. Loyalty comes when everyone knows each member of the team is doing their part. As a leader, it is your responsibility to hold your subordinate team accountable to the standards of work you set. When these standards are tough, but reasonable and attainable, your team will rise to the challenges you set for them.

Establish Self-discipline

3-4-71. Self-discipline is a key value that a leader must have, and it is a key value that he will expect from his subordinate team members. Self-discipline is an attitude that pushes you and your team to success. When you are self-disciplined, you maintain control of your emotional and physical state. Self-disciplined people are respectful, show up on time, and do their jobs to the best of their ability all the time.

Establish Respect

3-4-72. In paragraph 3-4-60 it was mentioned that we have diverse value systems in our society. As someone who will be leading your team into the future, you must realize that *people are your greatest resource.* So you have to learn to deal with the diversity of your followers. You should actively seek out opportunities to learn what makes each member of your team unique. This will help you to understand their point of view and to respect them.

3-4-73. The difficult part is to respect everyone's views and values, while at the same time holding them accountable to the overall goals and missions of your organization. You have to establish clearly what is expected of your followers. You do not have to be mean in your tone or actions; it is important to instruct your team in such a way that is not harsh or demeaning. Give instructions in a tone that motivates and inspires followership. When your followers feel you are respecting them, they will in turn respect your leadership.

3-4-74. I once had a student suggest to me that leading soldiers in the Army was "way easier" then leading civilians. He suggested "civilians don't just take orders." This comes from a mischaracterization of what it is like to be an Army leader. Rarely does an Army leader issue a direct order. It is seldom necessary to do so because you have earned your subordinates' respect and loyalty. When it is necessary to issue an order, your subordinates follow those orders because you have earned their trust. The same is true for you. If you have to "give orders" to get people to do their jobs, you are failing as a leader because you are losing the respect of your team.

Establishing Personal and Moral Courage

3-4-75. As a young leader who is not in the military, you may not believe you need to establish personal courage for yourself or your team. However, personal courage is not reserved for soldiers. Certainly, personal courage is a heavy burden in the Army; as a soldier you are expected to have both physical and moral courage. Courage is not an absence of fear; rather it is the ability to put fear aside and do what you know is right.

WO1 Thompson at My Lai

On March 16, 1968, helicopter pilot Warrant Officer (WO1) Hugh C. Thompson, Jr. and his two-man crew were on a reconnaissance mission over the village of My Lai in the Republic of Vietnam. WO1 Thompson watched in horror as he saw an American soldier shoot an injured Vietnamese civilian. Minutes later, when he observed American soldiers advancing on a number of civilians in a ditch, WO1 Thompson landed his helicopter and questioned a young officer about what was happening on the ground. When the officer told him that the ground action was none of his business, WO1 Thompson took off and continued to circle the area.

When it became apparent that the American soldiers were now firing on civilians, WO1 Thompson landed his helicopter between the soldiers and the group of ten villagers who were headed for a homemade bomb shelter. He ordered his gunner to train his weapon on the approaching American soldiers and fire if necessary. Then he personally coaxed the civilians out of the shelter and airlifted them to safety. WO1 Thompson's radio reports of what was happening were instrumental in bringing about the cease-fire order that saved the lives of more civilians. His willingness to place himself in physical danger in order to do the morally right thing is a sterling example of personal courage. (US Army Leadership FM 2-39)—*Illustration 18*

3-4-76. Physical courage is about overcoming the fear of bodily harm to do your job and lead others. It takes physical courage to jump out of an aircraft in Air-born School to become Air-born qualified. Physical courage is also what allows a police officer or fire-fighter to do their jobs. It takes physical courage as a health care professional to help patients that have infectious diseases. Show me any worker building a modern sky-scraper and I will show you physical courage; just think about what it takes to work hundreds of feet in the air.

3-4-77. Moral courage is your willingness to stand up for your values when it is most difficult. Moral courage is often overlooked as leaders establish value systems for their organizations. Moral courage enables you do the right thing regardless of the consequences, as was the case for WO1 Thompson in Illustration 18.

3-4-78. More often moral courage is expressed as candor. Candor means being outspoken, being frank, speaking honestly without hiding your intentions. Candor is calling things like you see them without concern for the possible uncomfortable consequences. You see something that is just not right and you cannot be quiet.

3-4-79. A word of caution when it comes to candor. Candor does not mean you just speak your mind all the time. You cannot go around telling people what you think they need to hear "for their own good." Candor requires respect of and trust in your team members. Candor takes diplomacy and sensitivity. Candor requires a leader to use an appropriate tone of voice and a motivating attitude so that when you speak you have earned the right to be heard.

I Got Fired

As a young Captain, I was assigned to command the Army's largest rifle marksmanship training facility. This had been a job reserved for senior Captains or Majors. I was honored and a bit overwhelmed. But I had an amazing team of soldiers under my command. One of my first assignments was to install the newest state-of-the-art computerized range. This range was going to significantly advance our ability to train soldiers. However, not everything was in order.

I quickly realized that my problem was not the new high-speed range we were installing. The biggest problem was that much of the rest of the training facilities were on the verge of having significant malfunctions. We were getting the job done but our ability to do so was going to become a major problem within that eighteen months.

I had to develop a solution. So I started to gather some important data. I collected current and past work order requests and target mechanism repair reports. I researched the current computer systems we were using and their failure rates. We were going to be faced with a target shortage for our older ranges because no one was manufacturing replacements targets. Once I had gathered all the necessary documentation, I went to my superiors.

Much to my dismay and disbelief I was blamed for the problems. Prior commanders had not had a problem taking care of business, so what was my issue and why was I failing to lead?

My issue was that the prior commanders were either not aware of the problems, or worse, did not have the moral courage to deal with them.

My immediate superiors' solution was to replace me. *I got fired.* I was sent to supervise the installation of the newest range and told to stay out of everything else. I was devastated; this could even have ended my career. Looking back, I thought that maybe I should have done what everyone else had done and just made sure we were getting by. But that is not who I am.

Just two months later, the Army's largest rifle marksmanship training facility started to have issues. These issues were not noticed by most, but they started negatively affecting our overall ability to train soldiers. The commander who replaced basically had no solution. He decided to place the blame on the soldiers assigned to the ranges. However, it is poor leadership to blame everyone else for what you are responsible for. He was replaced.

I was called back into my superior's office, reinstated as commander of rifle marksmanship, and told to "fix the problem." Within three months we had a working solution. It had required significant planning and implementation structures, but my team and I fixed the problem.—*Illustration 19*

3-4-80. Illustration 19 is an example of the kind of situation you might face as a young leader in the civilian workplace. You may find yourself dealing with a broken work environment where you and your team do not have what they need to get the job done. You may find yourself in a position where your superiors ask you to compromise your own values. Not all work environments have the values we wish they had, and many companies participate in dishonest practices. As a leader, you may find that your followers look to you to have the moral courage to do the right thing. It will take candor, and doing the right thing may even cost you your job, but your integrity and character will remain intact. As a leader you will be faced with some difficult choices; how you handle those choices will determine the quality of leader you will be.

"Always do everything you ask of those you command."
—General George Patton

Part Three, Section 4

INTEGRITY
Discussion Questions

1) How does the author define Integrity?

_____

_____

2) How does the author define Character?

_____

_____

3) In your own words, describe the difference between Integrity and Character.

_____

_____

_____

_____

4) How important is it for you as a leader to be seen as a person of Integrity?

1	2	3	4	5

1= Not important at all
2= Somewhat important
3= Important
4= Very important
5= The highest priority

5) If you are in a leadership position, do you think it's fair for other people to judge your ability to lead based on what you do or don't do during your 'off-duty' life?

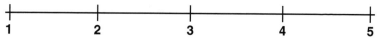

| 1 | 2 | 3 | 4 | 5 |

1= Totally not fair. When I'm off duty, what I do is my business.
2= Maybe if I'm doing something "wrong."
3= Not really fair but I understand why people think this way.
4= It's somewhat fair.
5= Absolutely fair; you cannot turn off your integrity.

6) Discuss why you think this way.

_____

_____

7) The author stresses that one way you as a leader learn to be *under* command before you can be *in* command is to lead "selflessly." To lead selflessly is to lead without the expectation of return or reward. Do you think this is possible for you?

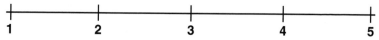

| 1 | 2 | 3 | 4 | 5 |

1= No way. If there is no reward, why do it?
2= I'm going to expect something for my efforts most of the time.
3= Possible with some effort.
4= I can do this some of the time.
5= Not only is it possible, I'm already doing it.

8) Review Illustration #17. Do you think the students had earned the right to reserve seats for themselves?
  Yes or No

Discuss your answer.

_____

_____

_____

_____

9) Have you ever had someone in a leadership position above you who lacked integrity and character?

Yes or No

Briefly describe the situation.

_____

_____

Discuss if it was easy or hard for you to follow this person.

_____

_____

Discuss what the morale was like for you and the rest of the team. Was it positive or negative and why?

_____

_____

Did the example of the leader you are discussing make you want to be like them or did it make you want to lead differently?

_____

_____

_____

Part Three: Section 5

B.A.S.I.C. Student Leadership CHOICE

Tactical Skill

3-5-81. Tactical skills are a leader's ability to take action and to make choices. The Army expects its leadership to make choices appropriate to the leader's level of responsibility and experience. Tactical skills are amplified by a leader's experience and by his mastery when it comes to soft skills, technical skills, integrity and attitude.

Experience

3-5-82. Experience is the number one factor that affects your ability to make quality choices and decisions. Experience, or the lack thereof, is the number one reason young leaders like you make the biggest mistakes. Young leaders believe they can make quality choices even when they lack the necessary experience to do so. Experience is the culmination of knowledge and skill we have acquired, based on our previous exposure to similar situations. You are the sum of your knowledge and experiences.

3-5-83. Since experience is so important to your ability to make quality choices, it is vital we give you opportunities to gain experience. In the Army we call this 'a training environment.' Unlike other models of leadership you can study, the Army is the one leadership model that consistently places *all levels* of leadership in training so they gain experience in making choices. Often the training environment is stressful, but training allows leaders a safe environment in which to make mistakes.

3-5-84. There is a saying I am sure you have heard: "We learn more from our mistakes than we do from our successes." Until recently, I would have completely agreed with this statement, but I think this saying is misunderstood. Yes, I have certainly learned a lot from my mistakes, but the key to learning from your mistakes is to *evaluate* where you failed, and unless you do so you have just failed again.

3-5-85. I believe that I have learned way more from my successes than my failures. We actually put more effort into our successes than our failures. Your successful experiences lead you into the future. When your choices, decisions and actions are successful, you are likely to repeat them in the future. Failure is the end of a process. We only learn from our failures if we actively choose to do so. If we choose not to, we will make the same mistakes over and over.

Leadership Failure

The Army has a long list of training schools that provide soldiers, at every level of command, the opportunity to train in an environment that allows learning from your mistakes. The key element in each school is that there is an *evaluation process*. This process takes each individual and walks them through the choices and decisions they have made. Senior leadership assists subordinate team members in understanding where they went wrong and, most importantly, how to fix it.

Leaders are allowed to make mistakes; no one is perfect. Failure is all part of gaining experience. Senior leadership expects that you will learn from your mistakes and not make the same mistake twice.

The lowest rank for an officer is 2nd Lieutenant (2LT). A 2LT is allowed to make errors in judgement. This is expected because of their lack of tactical skills. As a 2LT you are expected to make mistakes and gain experience at the same time. As you advance in rank, mistakes that a 2LT would make are not tolerated.

As a Captain (CPT.), two levels higher in rank, you are not expected to make the mistakes of a 2LT. You should have learned from your mistakes and the mistakes of your fellow officers. However, a CPT. is allowed errors in judgment that are appropriate for his leadership level, and this process continues as you are promoted to higher levels of command.—*Illustration 20*

3-5-86. Lack of experience is the biggest factor in students making mistakes. Not just students in leadership but every student. Often young leaders are unwilling or afraid to ask for help. We have a tendency to think that asking for help is a sign of weakness, when in fact it is a sign of maturity. Maturity allows you to judge the situation you are facing and to recognize you lack the experience to make the correct choice, so you seek assistance. As a leader, when you find yourself in a situation where you lack experience, ask for help.

Judgement

3-5-87. Judgement is your ability to "size up" a situation. Good judgement is the ability to size up a situation quickly, determine its importance, consider alternatives, and take correct decisive action. As a leader you need to also be clear on the consequences of what you are about to do. Each action you take affects personnel, equipment, and the goals of your organization. As you experience the positive results of having good judgment, your self-confidence will increase.

Decision Making

3-5-88. Typically, we think of choices and decisions as being the same. But it is important to understand the differences when we consider the ramifications of how we all go about living our lives. Decisions and choices are not the same, though they are unquestionably linked. Rarely does one happen without the other, though it is possible. Both the decision making and choice making processes are known to happen rapidly; often they happen so rapidly it seems instantaneous. Conversely, choices and decisions can also move along at a slow pace, making you wonder if you will ever accomplish anything.

3-5-89. Decisions require an active mental process. The US Army FM on leadership's definition of decision making: "Decision making is knowing *whether* to decide, then *when* and *what* to decide. It includes understanding the consequences of your decisions." The *what* to decide becomes the choices you have as a result of the decision making process. Choices are an opportunity for making a selection between one or more options. These options can be commonplace or can have life-altering results; they can be mundane or magnificent.

3-5-90. Army leaders follow two decision making processes at different leadership levels. The lowest is the troop leading procedures and at higher levels the military decision making process. However, let's simplify the decision making process down to these six basic steps:

The Six-Step Decision Making Process
1) Define the situation, problem, or option
2) Identify the available solutions/alternatives
3) Evaluate the identified alternatives

4) Make a decision

5) Implement the decision

6) Evaluate the decision.

3-5-91. Decision making is both a science and an art. It's a science because decision making can have very specific quantifiable results. Most corporations will tell you that they have to have a decision-making process in place. Decision making is also an art. I'm sure you know someone who just seems to have a knack for making decisions and making them well. Others of us can't even decide what to have for dinner. No matter your skill level at making decisions, you are faced with the process on a daily basis.

3-5-92. "Every once in a while, you may come across choices that are easy to make: yes or no, right or left, on or off. As you gain experience as a leader, some of the choices/decisions you find difficult now will become easier. But there will always be difficult decisions that require imagination, that require rigorous thinking and analysis, or that require you to factor in your gut reaction. Those are the tough decisions, the ones you are getting paid to make." (US Army Leadership FM)

Rules of Choice

3-5-93. Leadership is influencing others. With the choices you implement, you are influencing others. So as a leader you must realize there are rules to the choices you make.

Rule One: Bad News Does Not Get Better With Time

Strong leaders know they must own the choices they make. If you have done the hard work of following the decision-making process, most of the choices you make will turn out well. These choices are easy to take on. However, there are times when you choose poorly and things do not turn out as you planned. When this happens you must be the first to recognize the error and be totally clear about your role in the choices that were made. This becomes an element of your *character* and *integrity*. You cannot hide errors in judgement. When things go wrong, come clean and do not withhold information.

Rule Two: Choices Build Upon Themselves

The choices you make are not independent of other choices; they are building blocks for future choices. No choice is completely independent of other choices. It is vital as a student leader to understand that the choices you make today shape what kind of leader you will be in the future. Your choices are a reflection of your character and integrity. Choices made today will shape what happens tomorrow.

Rule Three: Choices Have Results

This rule is generally straightforward. My experience is that most students are making relatively good choices most of the time. Making good choices brings positive results. As the leader, your positive choices advance the mission and goals of your organization in a positive way.

However, there are times when the results of your choices turn out poorly. As stated in Rule One, you have to take responsibility for the poor choices you make. Poor choices will result in negative consequences. These consequences may require a minor correction or they may require significant changes. **(See 3-5-94)**

Rule Four: Choices Affect Others

If you are going to lead others, you must always remember that the choices you make affect others. You cannot say or believe "What I do shouldn't matter to anyone else." What you do and say does matter. We established this back in Section 1. As a leader, even the smallest choices you make have an effect on your team. If you want the influence that comes with leadership you have to sometimes make choices that go against *your* best interest but are in the best interest of your followers. That is true leadership.

Rule Five: With Increased Choice Comes Increased Responsibility

As a leader, when you demonstrate your ability to make appropriate choices, you will be given the opportunity to make more choices. The more consistent you are in making quality choices, the greater the value you and your choices have. Your choices will reflect your ability to take on increased responsibility.

Rebounding from Poor Choices

3-5-94. We all make mistakes. Learning to rebound from those mistakes is vital. Here are three tips to help you rebound from your mistakes.

1. Evaluate and Move Forward: As mentioned earlier, we only learn from our mistakes if we take the time to actively evaluate what went wrong and why. Rebound by identifying where in the decision making process you failed. Perhaps you identified the problem incorrectly or misunderstood the alternatives. Perhaps you had choices that seemed equally as good as others, but they weren't. Maybe you lacked the experience to make the decision on your own, in which case ask yourself if you should have sought advice to help make the decision.

2. Poor Choices Are Not Personal: Everybody makes poor choices. Just because you or a member of your team makes a mistake or messes up does not mean you/they are a failure. It means you/they are human. If you are not making a poor decision occasionally, you're not trying hard enough. Rebound by cutting your team some slack. Do not allow the mistake to become a personal failure. Reinforce your confidence in your team by focusing on the future, not the past.

3. Take Responsibility: Recognizing your role in what went wrong is vital. Rebound by accepting correction. True leaders are humble and realize that others have more experience and they can help you move forward and avoid making the same mistakes. Value those appointed above you.

3-5-95. Take advantage of the training environments you have available to you now. As mentioned earlier (3-1-5), most schools have Career Technology Student Organizations. You can also participate in student councils, student government, sports and clubs. These are great programs that will allow you to gain leadership experience, make mistakes and learn from those mistakes.

After- Action Review (AAR)
3-5-96. The after-action review is an outstanding tool that every young leader like you should incorporate into their leadership skills. Making the AAR part of your standard procedures after every major event, task, mission or training will set you apart

from every other young leader. The AAR will be a tool you will use throughout your career, no matter the career you choose.

3-5-97. The after-action review is just that: a review after an action. The AAR should be used as an opportunity to develop your subordinate team members. The AAR is there to answer these questions: how did we do, what did we do right, and what did we do wrong? The best AARs start even before the operation date because you plan with the AAR in mind.

3-5-98. As an organizational leader, you use the AAR to develop your team members by looking closely at whether they were able to do their jobs well. You give your followers a chance to talk about how they saw things. You want to know what they think went well, and what they think needs to be improved on so they can do their jobs better. You allow them to identify what they see as the successes and failures of the operation, task, mission or event. The goal is to look at the overall performance of the team.

3-5-99. As a subordinate leader, you want to get more specific about the details of how individuals performed in their specific areas, including yourself. This is where you offer leadership guidance to the team and one-on-one evaluation. The key in the process is that, as the leader, you do more lessoning than talking.

3-5-100. The AAR process should tell you what you did well and what you need to improve on. If you pay close attention to this information, it will assist you in making sure you repeat your victories and avoid your failures. Often we repeat the same events or tasks over and over again, and we always think we will remember the details but we typically don't. That is where the AAR comes in. You take notes and keep records of your successes and failures. Then you refer to the AAR's you collect over time. You will be amazed at how much more efficient you and your team become.

(See Appendix for a simple AAR.)

"A good solution applied with vigor now is better than a perfect solution applied tomorrow."
—General George Patton

Part Three, Section 5

CHOICE
Discussion Questions

1) Do you think your lack of experience is the number one reason you make mistakes?

1= Nope, not the reason I make most of my mistakes.
2= Sometimes but not always.
3= Sure, I'll buy that.
4= I agree that most of the time it's my lack of experience.
5= Completely agree.

2) Discuss why your level of experience is so important to how you make choices.

_____

_____

_____

3) Do you agree that you learn more from your mistakes than you do from your successes?

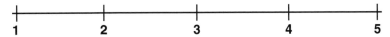

1= Totally agree. I learn more from my mistakes.
2= Somewhat agree.
3= I learn an equal amount from both.
4= I'm starting to learn more from my successes than my failures.
5= Disagree. I learn more from my successes.

4) In your own words describe the difference between a choice and a decision.

_____

_____

5) The author lists five rules of choice (3-4-92). Which of these rules do you have the most difficulty with and why?

_____

_____

_____

_____

6) When people make poor choices, do you believe they deserve a second chance?

```
+------------+------------+------------+------------+
1            2            3            4            5
```

1= Never deserve a second chance.
2= Sometimes they do.
3= Depends on if their poor choice affected me.
4= Most of the time they deserve a second chance.
5= Always deserve a second chance no matter what.

7) Think of a time when you made a poor choice and write it down.

_____

_____

8) Was making the choice you made caused in part by your lack of experience?
    Yes or No

Discuss your answer.

_____

_____

9) Being totally honest, did you take full responsibility, or did you try to blame others for your mistake?

_____

_____

10) Discuss how you felt at the time. Did you feel like you had failed?

_____

_____

11) Were you given a second chance?
   Yes or No

   Discuss your answer.

_____

_____

12) General George Patton served as a commander in WWII. One of his most famous quotes is: "A good solution applied with vigor today is better than a perfect solution applied tomorrow."

   What do you think General Patton is saying to leaders about making quality choices?

_____

_____

Pvt. Sharp
A Story of Triumph

I would like to echo what I said in the introduction before telling you the story of Pvt. Sharp.

The Army has a long history of producing great leaders. The Army leadership model is known to be a superior leadership training system, and this system produces above average leaders from average men and woman. Pvt. Sharp is one example of many.

I was a 1st Lieutenant (1LT) in command of a basic training company. My company consisted of 15 Drill Sergeants (DS) and a few administrative personnel. We had just received 200 female trainees. When I was in command of this unit, every soldier went through the same training. However, male and female soldiers were trained separately.

Basic training is a shock to everyone. It is both mentally and physically challenging. The first few days of training are about orienting a new recruit to the military system. Soldiers learn how to wear their uniforms, march as a unit, do physical training (PT), and master the other fundamental skills of a soldier. It really is not that difficult. You have to allow recruits to acclimate to being soldiers, and most soldiers start to fit in quickly after just a few days. But this was not the case for Pvt. Sharp.

"Pvt. Sharp, tears may have worked for you in your civilian life. But they aren't going to work for you today. So what is your malfunction, Sharp? Why are you here?"

She repeated herself: "I made a mistake."

"Sharp, if that's all you have for me...get out of my office."

93

Pvt. Sharp was having trouble fitting into the Army way of life.

• • •

Only a few days into training, DS Williams brought Pvt. Sharp to my office. DS Williams was the best Drill Instructor I had. We had been working together for close to two years and he had never brought a soldier to my office for counseling. So this meant that Pvt. Sharp was a special case and not in a good way.

I spoke privately with DS Williams about Pvt. Sharp. He said he had never encountered a soldier that was so unfocused, unmotivated, and completely distraught. He and the other DS could not seem to do anything to get Pvt. Sharp moving in a forward direction. She was basically non-compliant. She believed she had made a mistake and wanted to go home.

So I spoke with Pvt. Sharp again.

"Sharp, what is your malfunction? Why are you in my office?"

"I don't know," she said.

"What do you mean you don't know? You're wasting my time, Sharp. DS Williams says you can't seem to get with the program. Is he correct?"

"Yes, sir."

"So what's your problem, Sharp?"

"I think I made a mistake."

"What mistake is that, Sharp?"

"Joining the Army, sir. I think joining the Army was a mistake."

Now I'm getting irritated. "Pvt. Sharp, did you not freely raise your right hand and take an oath to serve your country? Were you not counseled on the seriousness of the commitment? Were you coerced in any way to join the Army?"

My questions were met with silence.

So I raised my voice slightly: "Sharp, did you hear me?"

Tears started running down her face.

"Sharp, tears may have worked for you in your civilian life. But they aren't going to work for you today. So what is your malfunction, Sharp? Why are you here?"

She repeated herself. "I made a mistake."

"Sharp, if that's all you've got for me…get out of my office."

She left.

DS Williams, First Sergeant Guevara and I decided we would look closely at her information and refer her for a psych evaluation. Several days later she received the evaluation and was found fit for duty.

Her malfunction was simple. She wanted to go home. Once you have joined the army, going home is not as simple as packing your bags and leaving. We were going to have to find a way of motivating Pvt. Sharp and molding her into a soldier.

With a little investigation I learned a great deal about Sharp's background. She came from a very well-off family in Connecticut. She had attended a private girls' academy where she graduated at the top of her class. Then Sharp was accepted to an Ivy League college where she failed out. Luckily for her, she was accepted to and attended another Ivy League college, but again she failed out. She had held several decent paying jobs in the last several years, all of which she had quit. Then she returned to college and was barely getting by.

Her father had apparently given her an ultimatum: Go to school, pick a major and make significant progress towards graduation; or get and keep a job. If she could not do so, he would cut her off financially. She failed and he cut her off.

Sharp had no direction, no goals, and no idea what to do with herself. Her friends were moving on with their careers and had gotten married and started lives of their own. Sharp became everyone's couch buddy and no one likes a couch buddy for long.

So apparently Sharp decided she would join the Army just to piss everybody off, especially her father. That didn't seem to be working, and now she was *my* problem.

We were three weeks into training and Sharp was still not performing to standards. DS Williams was tired of dealing with her attitude and her tears, and late one afternoon he again brought her to my office.

DS Williams said to me: "Sir, just send her home. I'm tired of dealing with her and she is bringing the entire platoon down. Get rid of her."

I asked her: "Pvt. Sharp, what am I supposed to do with you?"

At that moment, Sharp crumpled onto the floor in a fetal position and started wailing and crying. "I want to go home!" This was no ordinary crying fit. She was going all out—tears, moans, snot out of her nose, yelling—it was total hysteria.

"I want to go home…I want to go home!" she cried over and over.

My reaction: I sat down in my chair, reached behind my desk and picked up a box of tissue. Then I started tossing them, one at a time, over the front of my desk. The tissues began to pile up around her.

"Sharp, when you quit throwing your tantrum, we'll talk."

Both DS Williams and First Sergeant Guevara thought I had lost my mind. Was I really going to just let this soldier lie on the floor and pitch a fit like a child? Yup, that was my plan. I was not going to give her what she wanted because of her behavior. I was willing to and had the power to send her home, but not like that.

As the tissues started to pile up one by one on the floor all around Sharp, she just kept crying and wailing. So it dragged on. Both of my men were rapidly losing patience with me and with Pvt. Sharp.

Pvt. Sharp finally took a break to collect herself.

I went on the offensive. "Pvt. Sharp (voice raised), get off my floor now! I'm tired of your wailing, so stop!" She stood up.

Then I offered her the best motivational speech I had at the time.

"Pvt. Sharp, if you quit the Army, you're going to be a quitter the rest of your life."

I know…totally motivating, right? I looked over at DS Williams and he just shook his head at me as if to say "Is that all you can come up with?"

I started to ask Sharp questions.

"Pvt. Sharp, why did you join the Army? What were you expecting when you got here? You do realize the Army is not a place to hide from your problems?

What I learned from our conversation was that Pvt. Sharp had never felt like she fit in anywhere. She didn't have any idea what she wanted to do with her life. She envied all of her friends that knew exactly what they wanted to do. Sharp did not feel like she was good at anything. Pvt. Sharp felt lost and alone.

So I came up with a plan. A plan that made DS Williams think I was crazy.

"Pvt. Sharp, you are 27 years old. Do you realize that you are almost two years older than I am?"

She looked at me with complete disbelief.

"That's right Sharp, you're older than me."

You may not realize that most soldiers join the Army between the ages of 18 and 22. Sharp's age made her the grandma of the company. Other younger soldiers were looking up to her simply because of her age, and she didn't know it. That was part of DS Williams' problem with Pvt. Sharp; she was setting a poor example for the younger soldiers. He needed her to step up and lead the younger soldiers and not bring them down with her attitude. Or he needed to get rid of her.

"That's right, you're older than I am Sharp, and you can't even take care of yourself."

So I decided to try something different. I was going to put Pvt. Sharp in charge of other soldiers.

"Sharp, DS Williams is no longer going to get on your case for what you fail to do; he is going to hold you responsible for what *others* you are in charge of fail to do. *I'm* going to ride your case for what *you* fail to do."

"But that's not fair, sir. Why should I have to be responsible for anyone else?"

"Sharp, it's called leadership. Maybe, just maybe, you need to be responsible for something greater than yourself. I'm going to start by making you responsible for helping your squad buddies meet the physical training (PT) standards."

Pvt. Sharp was not a total disaster. She was in good physical shape. She was tall, about 5'10", lean and strong. Her first physical fitness test had gone well. The Army physical fitness test consists of pushups, setups and a two-mile run. Sharp scored 100% on pushups and setups, and almost maxed the run as well. This is highly unusual for a new recruit of either gender, and it gave us a place to start. She had also been a crew member; she had been on the rowing team all though school and continued to row as a workout. Sharp was an athlete and we made sure she owned it.

Pvt. Sharp started running with the slower running group to motivate her buddies. She spent time helping her buddies work on their upper body and core strength. Pvt. Sharp had someone else to take care of and it seemed to be working.

DS Williams made her a full squad leader. The very first step in small unit leadership that a soldier can take in the Army is to become a basic training squad leader. Within two weeks Sharp was starting to excel in other areas. She qualified as an expert basic rifle marksman and scored 100% on her physical fitness test. She continued to accept her leadership role as she assisted the other squad leaders.

Pvt. Sharp was rapidly learning what it meant to *come under command before she could be in command.*

Pvt. Sharp was on the path to becoming a leader. For the first time she had taken responsibility for her behavior. She started to walk tall and feel a since of pride. She had taken command of her attitude. Sharp knew she was accountable for what she had experienced in the past. Instead of seeing herself as a victim and a failure, and blaming others for the choices she'd made, Sharp learned to own her past failures and look towards the future. Pvt. Sharp had started to master a new set of skills including leadership skills. Most importantly she was on the path of success. She had gained new confidence in herself and her future was looking bright.

One of the best parts of being in command of this unit was that I had the ability to select several soldiers for promotion. It was a small promotion but it did come with benefits. I selected Pvt. Sharp for promotion. Because of her college credits and her performance in basic training, I was able to promote her to Specialist (SPC). She actually skipped being a Private First Class (PFC). This was no small action; it made a significant statement about SPC Sharps' leadership ability.

We held the promotion ceremony and we shipped these new Army soldiers off to their next training assignments' assessments. SPC Sharp was on her way.

It isn't often that years later you have the opportunity to hear the rest of someone's story. Fortunately, I had the pleasure of crossing paths with SPC Sharp again.

About two years after leaving my command in basic training, I was assigned command of Basic Rifle Marksmanship. One afternoon as I was leaving my office, a soldier in dress blue uniform was coming up the sidewalk towards my office.

It was highly unusual for anyone to just drop by my office since it was located several miles from the main post, and there was definitely no reason to see someone in their dress blue uniform. Yet, walking up the sidewalk was a female 2nd Lieutenant (2LT). 2LT is the lowest rank of an Army officer. She had to be lost.

She walked directly up to me and stopped. She saluted sharply and said; "Captain Grooms, do you have a moment to speak with me?"

I returned her salute. Still puzzled as to why she was out on the ranges in her dress blues, I said: "Sure, how may I help you, Lieutenant?"

"Sir, I wanted to say thank you for…"

She couldn't finish because I interrupted her. Could this possibly be the same soldier that was in my unit only a few years ago crying to go home? No possible way was this Pvt. Sharp. It was then that I glanced down to see her name tag. It read "SHARP."

"Pvt. Sharp...you have to be joking...you're an officer? What on earth happened to that soldier who thought she made a mistake joining the Army? Pvt. Sharp, you have got to be joking."

"No sir, no joke. It's *Lieutenant* Sharp now. I came here because I wanted to tell you in person how much I appreciate you for not giving in to me, for making me follow through on my commitment as a soldier. The day I graduated and you promoted me was the first time I ever felt like I had *earned* something. You made me feel successful. I wanted to personally express my appreciation to you for giving me an opportunity to lead others. It was the first time in my life that I realized that life didn't and shouldn't revolve around my wants and desires."

"Sharp, it was a major step to go to officer candidate school. What made you decide to become an officer?"

"Sir, I wanted to continue to develop my skills as a leader. What better place to do that than in the Army?"

"None that I know of, Lieutenant Sharp."

She and I chatted for just a few minutes before I had to leave for a meeting with my commander. But before we said our goodbyes, I had one more question.

"So Sharp, are you planning on making the Army a career?"

"Lord no! I still want to go home, sir. (We laughed.) I've just decided to wait a while."

She saluted and that was the last time I ever saw her. I can't imagine that she was anything less than wildly successful.

Summary

This manual has taken the battle tested Army model of leadership and provided you with the practical framework of B.A.S.I.C.

B. Behavior

A. Attitude

S. Skill

I. Integrity

C. Choice

Now that you are familiar with B.A.S.I.C. training, it becomes your responsibility to take charge of your behavior, recognize the power of your attitude, develop your personal and professional skills, be a person of integrity, and make quality choices.

Private Sharp did not see herself as a leader; nor was she excited about the prospect of having to lead anyone else. Yet when given the opportunity to lead, she stepped up, came under command, took charge of herself, and began to lead others.

I am confident that if you start to apply the wisdom contained in this manual, you will be prepared to lead not only yourself but others. As you come under command of these leadership lessons, your future as a leader is limitless.

Appendix

After Action Review (AAR) Sample

Here is a sample of the information that an AAR is trying to collect. This example will work well for student leaders putting on an event. Also, the AAR can be expanded or reduced based on your specific needs.

Before The Event

Event Title/Theme:
   What is your primary goal for the event?

Finances: (pay close attention to these records)
   Budget
   Expected income and payments

Dates:
   Include the start date and closing date.
   Include important dates such as leadership team arrival and departures.
   Deadline dates including all registrations.
   Alternate dates if available for "rainouts."

Times:
   Start and end times

Place:
   Physical location of the event, address, phone numbers

Contact Personnel:

Collect the title of the individual(s), their name, address, and office and cell phone numbers.

Collect names of anyone you speak to who makes decisions.

If you are inviting quests, speakers or presenters, collect all of their info as well.

Contracts:

Get everything in writing. A verbal promise is only good in writing.

Create an email folder and keep all email correspondence.

Keep all contracts on file.

After speaking with someone on the phone who agrees to do something or provide you with something, create a summary email of the conversation and send it to yourself and the person you spoke with.

Number of people expected to attend: and number actually in attendance.

Personnel List:

List all your team members and their responsibilities.

Supplies:

Listing your needed supplies is often a missed step. This step will save you lots of time and headaches because every year you think you will remember the stuff you need, but you never do. Have each member of your team create their own list and consolidate your lists. Your supplies list will grow to the point where you eventually have everything you need listed.

After The Event

Ask yourself and your team to consider the broad questions: What did we do right? What did we do wrong? Ask these questions for each of the areas below. As the leader, you need to listen closely to the answers your team gives you.

Finances:

Did you stay within your budget?

List both savings and unexpected costs.

Where can you save money? Where should you have spent more money?

Did you collect the expected income from your registrations? Should you increase or decrease the cost of the event?

Event Theme:

Was your theme appropriate? Did your audience "get it?"

Should we do the event again? Why or why not?

Did you achieve your primary goal?

What goals should you set for next year that you might have missed out on this year?

Was it fun? What can you do to make it better in the future?

What worked and did not work as far as achieving the goals for you event?

Dates:

Was the date you selected appropriate?

Did it conflict with other events that drew attendance away from your event?

Was the day of the week the best one possible for your audience?

If you changed the date/time of the year, would you increase attendance?

Did you receive your registration on time? If not, why, and can you improve on this?

Times:

Did you start and end on time? Why or why not? Can you improve on this?

Should you consider changing the times of events to better serve your audience?

Place:

Was the location appropriate for this event?

Did the location people fulfill their contract? Do you need to add elements to the contract?

Was the location too small or too big?

Did they have the necessary supplies and equipment for your needs? (stages, sound and video equipment, rooms, tables and chairs)

Did your attendees enjoy the facilities?

Did the event host at the location treat you and your attendees well?

If you were satisfied with the location, have you booked your next event?

Supplies:

What did you forget?

What did you bring that you did not need?

What would be a 'nice to have' in the future?

Review Team Members:

In general, did the team get the job done as expected?

Did you have everyone you needed? If not, who do you need to add?

Did you have too many people?

Did everyone have a job?

Did your team do their individual jobs? If not, how do you plan to deal with them?

How did they do their jobs? List areas of improvement and point out successes.

Did anyone try to 'steal the show' by putting themselves above the goals of the event?

After Action Reviews (AARs) are very specific to the event and to the information the leader is trying to collect. You may choose to focus on the overall success of the event; or perhaps it will be more helpful to focus on individual team member job performance. Or maybe you need to pay particular attention to the "beans and bullets" of the operation. As the leader, you decide on the goal of any AAR that you do.

"You are a leader, and you are an expert.
Don't let anyone tell you differently."
—Fred Grooms

You can find Fred Grooms on the Internet at:
www.fredgrooms.com
fred@fredgrooms.com

Made in the USA
Middletown, DE
20 May 2017